LIKE FATHER, LIKE SON
BASEBALL'S MAJOR LEAGUE FAMILIES

LIKE FATHER, LIKE SON
BASEBALL'S MAJOR LEAGUE FAMILIES

Sarah Gardiner White

SCHOLASTIC INC.
New York Toronto London Auckland Sydney

Acknowledgments

I would like to thank everybody who helped make this book possible, especially the Griffey family, the Ripken family, the Alomar family, the McRae family, the Javier family, the Stottlemyre family, the Tartabull family, the Alou and Rojas family, the Boone family, Harold Reynolds, Ken Brett, Chris Gwynn, Steve Sax, Nolan and Reid Ryan, Jim Samia, Dick Bresciani and the Boston Red Sox, Rich Griffin, John Maroon, Hector Martinez, Bobby Serrano, Gary Brown, Tom Mooney, Paul Ricciarini, Brian Goldberg, Debbie Larsen, John Traub, Kevin Kallal, Jay Horowitz, Craig Sanders, Mike Wilkens, George Koh, Molly Walsh, and Arthur Morris.

ISBN 0-590-46027-7

12 11 10 9 8 7 6 5 4 3 2   3 4 5 6 7 8/9

Printed in the U.S.A.   40

First Scholastic printing, July 1993

To Ellen, who took me to see my first Red Sox game in '86; to my mother, who made me go to that game; to my father, who talks baseball with me without getting bored; to my editor, for believing I could pull this off; to the rest of my family and friends; and especially to Gram, because she's great.

Contents

Introduction

Carrying On
the Family Name

It's not at all unusual for a family business to live on through generations. Corner grocery stores, laundromats, restaurants, and bookstores everywhere are often run by fathers and mothers, sons and daughters. At family gatherings, the son or daughter of a doctor might be asked about his or her plans to follow suit in the future. The child of a successful actor might grow up in the theatrical and cinematic industry and decide to go for the chance to get into the same field.

In highly skilled and artistic professions, success does not come easily. Popularity, *adequate* ability, and the family name will often hold for a while. But for how long? Certainly not forever, if excellence is to be upheld. The child of the professionally accomplished parent who is opting for the same career needs to have something more — a spark. This spark is often inherited; it consists of talent, intelligence, and dogged determination.

It takes a strong-willed individual to take over the family business, uphold the family name, *and* make a name for himself or herself. Often proud of their heritage, upbringing, and success, the off-springs in question may occasionally wish they could shed their surnames just long enough for people around them to see that, yes, they made it on their own.

In a few businesses, a lack of direction, skill, or aptitude may be overlooked, at least temporarily. If the son of a grocer works in the store after school, and puts bread at the bottom of customers' bags or fails to make change properly, chances are that his father will take him aside in order to set him straight. In other words, this younger kin often gets at least a second chance.

In the deeply competitive world of professional baseball, that simply cannot happen. There are too many talented, driven athletes trying to scratch and claw their way to the top. Slackers don't last and, of course, they usually don't even get to sign a contract. Baseball scouts are trained and experienced in spotting great initiative and a good work ethic as well as talent. They must take personality traits like laziness into account — sometimes overlooking *slight* lacks in ability. For example, why should a scout give a careless athlete the chance of a lifetime that a perhaps less-gifted but much more hardworking player deserves? Attitude is one of the most important things about a player that a scout can observe when he is on the road searching for tomorrow's pros. Accomplished major-leaguers all over America do have a crucial feature in common — the *spark*.

There are hundreds of minor and major league baseball players in the world. It is extremely difficult for a young, ambitious ballplayer to get to sign a professional contract with a major league organization. Admittedly, it is an incredibly exciting feeling to be hired by a real, honest-to-goodness team. But then, after a player arrives in a new city to play rookie ball, he finds that the challenge and hard work have only just begun. The ladder to the big leagues is a tiny, rickety one, crowded with players of all sizes, shapes, strengths, and weaknesses. Those with the most weaknesses don't get the great thrill of touching one of the top rungs. They are ruthlessly knocked off by stronger, better players. A talented young player destined for the major leagues has his work cut out for him. He must prove to his manager, coaches, teammates, and opponents that he is top-notch, hard-nosed, and ready to proceed to the next level.

The people in this book have all accomplished the most-difficult personal step in baseball. They have made it to the major leagues. Some of them have even been in the World Series, or the annual Major League All-Star Game. The sons of these famous fathers had the advantage of growing up within the baseball environment. But really, all that did was get them used to baseball life. It didn't guarantee any of them a job. While they were born with a recognizable name, the rest was up to them. They have made it to the big leagues, and they have themselves as well as their families to thank.

Like anyone else, a professional baseball player can fall on hard times, either in life or on the field. A good measure of his character is his ability to pick himself up after a fall. When a person's life is pretty much smooth sailing on an even keel, a lack of toughness may not be visible on the surface. In baseball, however, it doesn't work that way. As fun and glamorous as major league life seems to be, it is also a job that carries a great deal of pressure.

These major league baseball sons received early lessons about some of the stresses. But they really did not know how they would deal with these problems until they actually got to the major leagues.

In the following chapters, major league fathers and sons cordially took the time to talk about their lives and their careers. While each has a unique outlook, they all share one thing. They have all put in the hard work to accomplish their goal — to live their lives in the major leagues.

1
The Griffeys

Playing Side by Side

On August 31, 1990, players throughout the major leagues got into their uniforms and went out for batting practice before their games. Just another day. But things actually weren't so ordinary everywhere.

In the Seattle, Washington, Kingdome the Mariners were suiting up to play the Kansas City Royals. Just another day? Not really. Something very special was going to happen that night. Something that had never happened before. For the first time in major league history, a father and his son — 40-year-old Ken Griffey, Sr., and his 20-year-old son, Ken Jr. — were going to be part of the same lineup. Not only that, they would play right next to each other in the outfield. Ken Sr., who had already played for 18 years in the

The Griffeys talk shop on the field.

big leagues, was the left fielder. Ken Jr., a sophomore major-leaguer, was in center field.

Storm Davis was pitching for the Royals. Ken
Sr., in his first at bat, singled to center. Ken Jr.
followed with a single to right. Naturally, the
crowd went crazy, cheering hard for the two relatives.

Later that night, Ken Sr. happily told reporters
that it was the best thing that had ever happened
to him in professional baseball.

"This tops my career," Ken Sr. said in a press
conference following the game. "It was better
than the seventy-six batting race or my two

World Series. For me, playing with Junior is number one. I'm standing there in left field and looking over to center, and there's the same kid I've played with ever since he was knee-high."

"It was just a little weird, looking at him out there," said Ken Jr. "He told me that I looked like I was 12 years old until I walked up to him, and he had to look up at me!"

Ken Sr. is now a scout for the Seattle Mariners and the color commentator for the Mariner TV station. His last year in baseball was tough going for him because he suffered a herniated disc in his spine. However, he still fondly remembers playing alongside his son, and he admitted that it was a strange feeling to share the same profession — and the same *outfield* — with Ken Jr.

"I'm looking at this kid that I *raised*," recalled Ken Sr., "and he's out in center field, in the major leagues. Every once in a while, I'd get a flashback. But it was a lot of fun. I enjoyed every minute of it."

Ken Sr. is a veteran of the game. At the time, Junior wasn't. The whole idea of playing next to his dad was a bit overwhelming for him.

"When I got on the field," Ken Sr. explained, "I was able to concentrate and do my job. I could put a lot of things aside because I had played for so long. I had played for twenty-four years, but this was all new to him. It was a little harder for him because he was standing there thinking, *I'm playing with my Dad.* So he was more nervous than I was. I told him that he would be there for

Ken Griffey, Sr., is a veteran of baseball.

a long time, so he should just relax and play the game. It finally dawned on him about the last two weeks of September that that was what he should do. But the first couple of weeks, it was kind of tough for him."

The Griffeys, obviously, were a pair of outfielders who knew each other very well. Aside from the fact that each performed exceptionally well at his position, the communication was especially good. It was also clear that the two had an immensely good time together. During Mariners games, TV commentators would often point out the Griffeys jostling one another in the dugout, or smiling for the camera. Or during a pregame stretching session, Junior might gleefully knock his dad over. Ken Jr. is three inches taller than his father and he sometimes uses his size to his advantage. All in good fun, of course.

"I like to body slam off my father," explained Ken Jr. with a mischievous smile. "We wrestle a lot."

When all of the Griffeys are together, antics abound.

"Our house is like the Huxtables' when we're all together," said a grinning Ken Jr., who loves *The Cosby Show* and *In Living Color*. "Everybody's always laughing, making jokes with each other. And I get in trouble because I'm the practical joker in the family."

One vivid example of Ken Jr.'s tricks might come to the minds of baseball fans. During a game in September 1990, Ken Sr. stood in the

Ken Sr. at bat for the Seattle Mariners

outfield, called for a fly ball, and poised to make the catch. Suddenly, Ken Jr. could be seen playfully sprinting in front of his father to snatch the ball from under his nose. Senior rolled his eyes and laughed, and Junior raced away snickering all the while. The center fielder runs the show out in the pasture — even if he's your son.

"I was camped under the ball," Ken Sr. said, "and I told him. And he came across and took it. So, I was a *little* disturbed by it. *He* thought it was funny. That's when I really got kind of mad at him, because he started laughing at me. He said, you know, 'Let the sure hands have it.' And I wanted to choke him! I told him, 'Don't ever run across me again while I'm standing under the ball.'"

And, he hasn't. But the out was made, and the inning ended. So, it worked out for the moment. And Ken Sr. now remembers the incident with amusement. (And, no, Ken Jr. didn't get a fatherly swat in the clubhouse after the game.)

"But I told him I was taking the car keys," Ken Sr. said, "so he couldn't drive around that night!"

One week after the Griffeys first manned the Seattle ball field together, Ken Sr. was named the American League Player of the Week. From September 3 through 9, he hit .632 with one home run and seven RBIs. It was the first time in his career that he had won that honor. It was certainly a pleasant turnaround for a man who had been released only days earlier by the Cincinnati Reds.

And things kept on getting better. On Septem-

10

ber 14, 1990, the Mariners played the California Angels. In the first inning, Ken Sr. hit a homer off of the Angels right-handed Kirk McCaskill (now with the Chicago White Sox). Ken Jr. was right behind him in the lineup. After Senior ran the bases, he met up with his son as he crossed the plate. Then he went to the dugout and waited to see what his son would do. After taking three balls, Ken Jr. punched the ball over the left-field wall. As he circled the diamond, he was *literally* following in his father's footsteps. When Junior got back to the dugout, he and his dad embraced for one of the happiest baseball hugs ever.

It's easy to see where Ken Jr. inherited his great talent. Senior has been known to go barreling into — or practically over — the outfield wall to rob an opponent of a home run. For example, in 1985 he kept Boston Red Sox second-baseman Marty Barrett from homering with a dramatic catch which ended with an acrobatic somersault. Nowadays, Junior can be seen doing the same thing. In fact, Ken Jr. has two Rawlings Gold Glove awards to date. Senior has been elected to play in three Major League All-Star Games (1976, 1977, and 1980). He also took part in the 1975 and 1976 World Series, in which the Cincinnati Reds defeated the Red Sox and the New York Yankees, respectively. Ken Sr. tied a National League Championship Series record in 1975 when he stole three bases in Game Two versus the Pittsburgh Pirates on October 5. He played in every game of the World Series

Ken Griffey, Jr., is one of baseball's most-popular players.

against Boston, batting .269 with four RBIs.

Five years later, Ken Sr. was named the Reds Most Valuable Player. He hit .294 that season with a career-high 85 RBIs. He was also the MVP in the 1980 All-Star Game. He got two hits, including a home run off New York Yankee pitcher Tommy John.

Senior became a Yankee himself following the 1981 season. His debut with the "Bronx Bombers" was outstanding. And he hit .340 with seven homers and had 29 RBIs in his final 38 games in 1982. It's really quite difficult for a hitter to maintain a .300 average or better for an entire season. But Ken Sr. accomplished just that in 1983.

By the time Ken Jr. was about 16 years old, he had decided that the career he wanted most was baseball. When he was much smaller, he and his brother Craig would get into their uniforms at around 6:00 in the morning in eager anticipation of the annual Father/Son games at their dad's ballpark.

"And then my mom would have to wash the uniforms before we went to the ballpark," Ken Jr. recalled with a smile.

Ken Jr. and Craig, now 22, were involved in sports all through school. They both graduated from Moeller High School in Cincinnati, Ohio, which has been rated the state's number one school. Ken Jr. played three years of football and four years of baseball. Craig was a football and track star. He played baseball as a child, but stopped playing it competitively when he was

Ken Jr. springs into action for the Seattle Mariners.

about 8 years old. Craig's football talent was so good that he received a scholarship to Ohio State University. By 1991, however, he had a stress fracture in his back and could not participate in the spring football practices. Meanwhile, his interest in baseball had become rekindled.

"He realized that baseball was much safer," Ken Jr. pointed out.

Ken Sr. was surprised and pleased when the Seattle Mariners drafted Craig in 1991. Craig batted .253 in 45 games with 20 RBIs in his first year at the Mariners' Tempe, Arizona, club. He is an outfielder like the other Griffeys. Time will tell how things will work out for Craig. But given his genes and athletic talent, he should be able to hold his own just fine.

"I didn't think Craig wanted to play baseball," Ken Sr. admitted. "But it turned out to be really good for him. He's learning. He's not like Junior, where a lot of things come more easily for him. Because he stopped playing when he was eight, this is all new to him. That's the only tough part. It's going to take him a little while to get [to the majors]."

So, both Griffey sons are pro ballplayers. They also have a 21-year-old sister, Lathesia, who lives in Oakland with her husband and their two children.

"I have a grandson and a granddaughter," Senior said proudly. "So, I'm doing fine!"

Ken Sr. was not the least bit shocked when his young namesake went the baseball route. "I wasn't surprised at all," Sr. said. "The only surprise I had is how quickly he got here to the big leagues. When he first started playing, he was seventeen. He went to Bellingham and he did so well there. And I said, 'Well, if they give him a shot at playing at the major league level, he won't go back.' And he really performed when he got to spring training, even the first year. Dick Williams (the Mariners manager from 1986 to 1988) was thinking about taking him then, at eighteen. It was a surprise, but it wasn't a surprise once he got there."

In 1989, Ken Jr. was only 19 years old. At spring training that year, he set Mariners spring training records by getting 33 hits, 21 RBIs, and having a 15-game hitting streak in 26 total games. He batted .359 with two homers. The new Mariners manager, Jim Lefebvre, was so impressed by him that he named him the starting center fielder for Opening Day. That first day, a jittery Ken Jr. ran out onto the field as his name was announced, praying that he wouldn't trip and fall in front of the crowd. He didn't. As a matter of fact, in his first at bat against the Oakland A's Dave Stewart, he hit a double. It was clear that this young man was in the big leagues to stay.

Junior has quickly evolved into one of the game's most-popular players. During his rookie year, a Ken Griffey Jr. chocolate bar was put on the market. Ken Jr. himself is allergic to chocolate, but luckily that was not the case for much of America. The candy bar is no longer sold, but at the time, sales soared. Ken Sr. still has a couple of them in his freezer, to keep as souvenirs.

"You've got to keep them frozen," Ken Sr. laughed.

Even though Ken Jr. shouldn't eat chocolate, he had to sample one of his candy bars. After all, they were named after him.

"He tasted it," Ken Sr. recalled, "and he suffered for it. He usually breaks out. And that was his problem, he was breaking out. And plus, he gets a little hyper when he gets sweets. Especially as a kid — oh, he wouldn't slow down! If he got any chocolate or candy, he'd be up all night. And

Ken Griffey, Sr., and his son Ken Jr. were the first major league father and son to be in the same lineup.

I had to be up all night with him."

So, Mr. and Mrs. Griffey made sure that Kenny didn't get anything sweet to eat after 6:00 at night.

"But now," Ken Sr. said with a grin, "he can do anything he wants."

Ken Jr. has been in three All-Star Games. He was the American League leading vote-getter in 1991. The following year, he played in the 1992 game, going 3-for-3 with a third-inning homer on a sinker pitch away thrown by Chicago Cubs pitcher Greg Maddux. (Greg, incidently, is part of a baseball family himself. He has a brother, Mike, who pitches for the San Diego Padres. The 1992 All-Star Game was in San Diego and Mike even let Greg use his locker for the event.) Ken Griffey and his dad became the first father/son combination to hit home runs in the All-Star Game. Ken Jr. was named the game's MVP, just like his father had been in 1980.

All ballplayers run into trouble now and again. That comes with the pro ball territory. But when Ken Jr. faced challenges in the minor leagues, he knew that good advice was just a phone call away. He spoke with Ken Sr., and also his mom, Alberta, often.

"I talked to him a few times," said Ken Sr. "He was struggling in his first year in Bellingham, and we talked about it. He told me what he was doing wrong, and I said, 'If you're doing that, then what should you do?' And I'd let him answer his own questions. You know, let him think it out for himself. He's the one who's going to have to make the adjustments at the plate. I mean, I can *tell him* what's wrong, or *tell him* what to do. But he *has to do* everything that it's going to take to get the job done."

Even now, their baseball conversations often happen the same way. But Ken Sr. pointed out that once they were playing together, they kept baseball on the field. When they left the ballpark, the subject would switch to non-baseball matters. When baseball is one's life, other ideas and interests are often a welcome change from the routine.

Baseball is Ken Jr.'s number one talent. But he has also had other pursuits to keep him busy. Like a lot of kids, school wasn't always his favorite place in the world. But he did enjoy math and science. Ken Jr. says that this is partially due to playing game after game of Yahtzee with his grandmother. She often beat him, and that pushed him to try harder.

"That's how I learned how to add so quickly," Ken Jr. explained. "And then, I got faster than she was."

Ken Jr. also took art the entire time he was in high school. Mechanical drawing was his favorite. He would like to be able to design his own house someday. The only class that didn't work out too well for Ken was chemistry.

"I got kicked out of chemistry," Ken Jr. recalled, with a guilty but good-natured expression. "I blew up the lab. I mixed something together and ten minutes later, it went all over the place. So, they said, 'You've gotta go.' "

Well, no one's perfect. But all in all, it's more than safe to say that the Griffey family is filled with accomplished people.

In 1989, the two Kens became the first father/son combination to play in the major leagues at the same time. Fans were pretty happy with that, and might have thought that the two of them playing together on the same team would never happen — that it might be too good to be true. But it came true. And that was more than good. It was downright great.

2
The Ripkens

Just the Family Business

The relatively new Oriole Park at Camden Yards in Baltimore, Maryland, is a wonder to see. Adorned with an old-fashioned charm, it seems to uphold everything that baseball should be. Oriole Park will be the site for the 64th Annual Major League All Star Game in 1993. But that's not the only thing that can make fans of the Baltimore area proud. Until the 1992 season, they could also watch a family baseball tradition right on the field of every home game — Cal Ripken, Jr., and his brother Billy.

Cal Jr. and Billy grew up in Aberdeen, Maryland, with Cal Sr., their mother, Vi (short for Violet), and their brother, Fred, and sister, Ellen. Cal Jr. and Billy showed their love for baseball early, especially Cal Jr. It's only fitting that they grew up to play for the nearby Orioles

The Ripken family is well-known to Baltimore Oriole fans.

once they made it to the big leagues.

Until 1992 when he retired, their father, Cal Sr., could be seen in the third-base coach's box, running through various signals that instruct players on how to run or hit. He worked directly with the manager, John Oates, who often made the decisions and then gave the cues to Cal Sr.

On the field, Cal Jr. and Billy take up the Orioles middle infield, playing shortstop and second base, respectively. Is it a strange feeling for the two brothers to be playing side by side in the infield? No way! They're so busy doing their jobs that before they know

Double trouble! Cal Ripken, Sr., and Jr. argue a call with the ump.

it, the inning is over and it's time to get ready to bat.

"It *is* kind of neat," admitted Billy one rainy day in Fenway Park when asked about working alongside his brother. "But the brother stuff goes right out the window once the game starts. I have a double play to turn, and he's got to get the ball to me. I know people find this hard to believe, but when the ball's hit, I don't look over there and say, 'Oh, my brother's going to give me the ball.' When we're out on the field, we don't look at each other that way."

The fact that the Ripkens both wear the same uniform means more to those who *watch* the game as opposed to those who are actually *playing* the game. They've been together so long, they don't know it to be any other way.

"It just seems like a natural thing," explained Cal Sr. in a 1992 interview. He was in the Orioles organization for 37 years as a player, coach, and manager. "They understand my job, and they were always well aware of what was going on."

Cal Sr. managed the Baltimore Orioles in 1987, and became the first father ever to manage two sons in a regular-season major league game. He has spent 15 years as part of the Orioles coaching staff. He managed from 1961 to 1974 in the Orioles

Cal Ripken, Jr., gets some TLC from mom while dad looks on.

minor league system — longer than any minor league manager in Orioles history.

When Cal Jr. was little, he used to take great joy in accompanying his father to numerous minor league games. All he had to do was look at Cal Sr. and his teammates, and he knew what he wanted to be.

"I didn't go to a lot of major league games," Cal Jr. explained. "I knew that major league baseball existed, but my only reference was what I was dealing with. It seemed like minor league baseball was the thing. When most kids say they want to be a baseball player, they mean they want to play in the big leagues. And I looked at the guys in the minor leagues as having the perfect job. I mean, they were playing a game and getting paid for it. The amount of money was irrelevant. Just the fact that they were playing, and that they could do that for their livelihood — that idea, I liked."

By the time Cal Jr. was 11, he had decided what he wanted. He found that his athletic skills were quite a bit better when compared to his peers, especially in baseball. But even though he showed such prowess at a young age, his father knew better than to get too enthusiastic too soon.

"I see so many young kids go out and play Little League," Cal Sr. explained, "and everybody gets all excited about them. But by the time they get to be sixteen or seventeen, they lose interest and don't pursue it. So, you're really not looking at that age group to see whether they're going to be professional players."

Of course, a promising young player can't even be signed to a pro contract until he is finished with high school. And that is precisely the point in time when Billy first saw a road ahead of him that could lead to the big leagues. He admittedly wasn't sure what he wanted to do in life when he was a teenager, which is pretty common among people that age. But when he got drafted by the Orioles, he decided to give it his all.

Things can be rough for a minor-leaguer when he's just starting out in pro ball. Cal Sr. could certainly empathize with that, and Billy took advantage of that fact, picking up the phone whenever he had problems with his game.

"You knew it was a baseball matter when my mother would pick up the phone and I'd said, 'Hey, Mom. Put Dad on,'" Billy said. "If I'd just called to talk, then Mom would stay on the phone."

But that doesn't mean that the women in the Ripken family don't offer some advice to the boys once in a while.

"They're a whole lot more informed about what goes on than someone who's not in it at all," Cal Jr. observed. "It's a little bit different talking to them about it. Sometimes that's good because they don't have the same perspective. Their opinions are not colored in any way. It's good to talk to my mom and my sister, just to get a different bit of advice."

Cal Jr. and Billy Ripken feel at home on the field.

Cal Jr. and Billy certainly save a lot of money on long distance phone calls now if they need baseball help from Dad, especially since he lives in the Baltimore area.

"When I have a baseball question," Billy said, "I don't hesitate to ask Dad. He's pretty much like a baseball encyclopedia."

"Sometimes, there are questions," Cal Sr. agreed. "Because I [was] a coach, I [would] talk to all of them at various times. Not because I'm the father, but because I [was] a coach."

Cal Jr. and Billy spend time together talking baseball, too. Many times, they sit in the club-house long after other players have gone home, just to hash out the details of the game. But, according to Billy, the baseball discussions stay in the locker room once the brothers leave. Then Cal Jr. returns home to his wife, Kelly, and their daughter, Rachel; and Billy goes home to his wife, Candace, and their two dogs — Aussie Blue, an Australian cattle dog, and Dawg, a husky.

Sometimes on the road, Cal Jr. and Billy go out together, maybe to grab a bite to eat after the game. Billy loves steak and potatoes, and Cal Jr. isn't too fussy. But they don't do this *every* night. Many times, each does his own thing. It might not be a good idea to be overexposed to each other, especially since they work together at close range.

Billy Ripken goes all out to make a play.

"But I don't think we've gotten sick of each other yet!" Billy said, with a grin. "It's just fun."

Cal Jr. pointed out that it's nice to have family around him, especially for those times when he is faced with a lot of pressure or needs to blow off a little steam.

"You do need people to talk to," Cal Jr. said. "In this life-style, Billy and Dad understand it, because they've both been in it. It gives you a chance to have people around who can help you solve problems."

As small boys, Cal Jr. and Billy often played games together, even though they are four-and-a-half years apart in age. They liked to invent their own sports. Tape ball was a Ripken favorite. The boys would make a small ball out of tape, and play a form of stickball using half of a broomstick as a bat. Cal Jr., being older, bigger and stronger, sometimes dominated the games, and that got Billy down.

"At times," Billy recalled, "it got pretty fierce at that level. He would always win, and I would always get mad."

So, yes, the Ripkens did square off on each other once in a while. But Billy was quick to point out that Cal Jr. was also a very loyal older brother. Nobody on the playground could pick on Billy — only Cal!

But basically, the four Ripken siblings got along very well. And to this day, Billy has a lot of good things to say about his big brother. In fact, he had trouble thinking of only one example of Cal Jr. making him especially proud to be his brother. "That could be any day," Billy said, shaking his head. "To watch him every day is something else. It's just the overall thing. He can *play*."

But of course, so can Billy. During the 1991 season, he was ranked second-best as the American League's defensive second baseman in a *Baseball America* poll conducted among league managers. (Roberto Alomar of the Toronto Blue Jays, another big-leaguer's son, came in first.) In 1990, Cal Jr. and Billy accounted for a meager total of only 11 errors. Later that season, on September 15, 1990, each Ripken brother hit a home run off Toronto's David Wells. That same season, Billy led the Orioles in three offensive categories: average (.291), doubles (28, in a tie with Cal Jr.), and sacrifice bunts (17, which tied for the league lead with Oakland's Mike Gallego, now the Yankees second baseman). Unfortunately, he was slowed down a bit by shoulder, back, rib, and ankle injuries and was only able to start 98 games. His brother Cal Jr. pointed out that Billy's playing style accounts for many of his injuries. Billy often goes all out to make a play and that's a valuable asset to any team.

The 1991 season worked out well for Cal Jr., to say the least. He finished the year with a .323 average, 34 home runs, 114 runs batted in, *and* the American League Most Valuable Player trophy. He also got the Rawlings Gold Glove for his position. He is well-known for having played more consecutive games than any living player. The man who holds the all-time record is the late Lou Gehrig, who played 2,130 consecutive games for the Yankees. Longevity is difficult to sustain in this game, since the injury factor is high for any player who goes out and plays hard every day.

In 1990, Cal Jr. made the fewest errors ever committed by a shortstop in one season — just three. Cal Jr. is an All-Star Game veteran. In the 1991 event in Toronto's Skydome, Cal hit a homer that allowed the American League to overtake the National League in a 4–2 victory. It's not too surprising that Cal Jr. started the 1992 All-Star

Cal Ripken, Sr., shakes his son's hand as Cal Jr. rounds third base.

Game after receiving a whopping 2,699,773 votes, the most for a player since Montreal's catcher Gary Carter got 2,785,407 votes in 1982.

At 6 feet 4 inches (the tallest regular shortstop in major league history), Cal Jr. looks more like a rangy, willowy outfielder. But his skill and quickness around the bag prove he is one of the finest shortstops in the game.

This understandably makes Cal Jr. one of the most-famous ballplayers around. He accepts his celebrity status and understands the responsibility he has to his fans. But at the same time, he feels sort of strange having people treat him so special. He sometimes wishes he could blend into the crowd and not be singled out.

"I don't perceive of myself as a superstar," explained Cal Jr., who also belongs to numerous charitable organizations. "I do know that people maybe look up to me, and they might think I'm more important or different than I actually am. But I believe that everybody's equal. I think that everybody has a special gift or talent that they're good at. It just might not be something they sell tickets to, or put on TV."

One can go on forever citing Cal Jr.'s accomplishments. His talent has been inherited, but his physical strength comes from a rigorous, disciplined training program, as well as a sensible diet. Cal Jr. is quick to admit that anyone can have a sweet tooth, including himself. But he tries to eat in a way that helps him give his best in every game.

When Cal Jr. went off to play rookie ball in Bluefield, West Virginia, his parents worried that he might not eat well. So his mom gave him a collection of simple recipes to take with him. Cal Jr. decided to follow his parents' advice. What if he ate poorly, and consequently performed terribly on the field? And there's no doubt that a person can feel just awful when he's not eating right.

"I'm not a nutritional fanatic," Cal Jr. explained. "From going away, I just got into the habit. To me, it's as though I'm a car, and what I put in is my fuel. And if you don't put the right fuel in, you can't function properly."

The Ripkens have many reasons to be pleased with all of their children. Ellen, the oldest, works in the office of a construction company in Baltimore. Fred, who is between Cal Jr. and Billy in age, works as a motorcycle repairman. Vi Ripken was honored in 1988 at the annual "Tops in Sports" baseball dinner as Maryland's "First Lady of Baseball." So, Cal Sr. has every reason to be happy about their well-rounded family, including Cal Jr. and Billy.

"We're very proud of their accomplishments, both on and off the field," Cal Sr. said, with a smile. "Someday I will reflect on those things. Maybe when I'm sitting in a rocking chair someday, I'll do that."

But for now, life as a Ripken — for all of them — will be business as usual.

3
The Alomars

An All-Star Tradition Begins

There is a beautiful town in southern Puerto Rico called Salinas, which overlooks the Caribbean Sea. Being close to the equator, Salinas can get pretty hot. It's a fortunate coincidence that two of today's hottest young players, Sandy and Roberto Alomar, grew up there. That is, when they weren't living in one of the major league cities where their father, Sandy Sr., played ball. Sandy Sr. had a 15-year major league career that took him and his family to Milwaukee, Atlanta, New York, Chicago, California, and Texas. Just like other big league families, the Alomar boys loved to go to the ballpark with their father, and they found a lot to do once they got there.

"We used to play paper-cup baseball in the stands," recalled Sandy Jr., who is now the All-Star catcher for the Cleveland Indians. "We didn't watch the game that much. We were so busy entertaining ourselves that we missed most of it."

Sandy and Roberto each received a small uniform that boasted the team colors of their father's team. Whenever their father went to another team, that meant Robbie and Sandy each got a new uniform.

"We wanted to be like our father," said the now 27-year-old Sandy Jr. with pride.

Both sons remember getting to know some of Sandy Sr.'s teammates, like New York Yankee greats player/manager Billy Martin and catcher Thurman Munson. Sandy Jr. remembers getting a few tips from Mike Hargrove when Mike and Sandy Sr. played for the Texas Rangers. Mike is now Sandy's manager in Cleveland, and Sandy stands a good five inches taller than Mike! It's funny how things work out.

When the Texas Rangers star pitcher Nolan Ryan was playing with Sandy Sr. for the California Angels, Roberto was pretty young. But he remembers how nice Nolan was to him. Around a decade-and-a-half later, Roberto got his first major league hit, a single, off of Nolan. It was also Roberto's first big league game. Nolan was pitching for the Houston Astros at the time. They talked about it the next day.

"He told me congratulations," recalled Roberto, who is now 25, "and said just to keep it up. He's one of the best I've ever seen."

Chances are that a lot of people in the baseball

Sandy Alomar, Sr., concentrates on the game.

circuit will be saying the same thing about Roberto for a long time to come. One person who feels that way today about both Alomar brothers is Nolan Ryan himself. Nolan remembers the days when little Robbie and Sandy raced around the ballpark while their father practiced.

"They were very active kids who were very involved in baseball," said Nolan. "So, it doesn't surprise me that both of them ended up in baseball. They were obviously blessed with good genetic athletic ability."

When Roberto signed in 1985, he went to play for the San Diego Padres Charleston club in South Carolina. This was when all of the Alomars

35

were with the Padres. It can be a difficult adjustment for a player to move away from home for the first time. But Roberto didn't have to worry about that. His father was coaching and his brother was playing for Charleston. So, the three of them shared an apartment. It was a nice time for them because they had the chance to be together.

"That was easy for all of us," Sandy Sr. said. "I just tried to teach them the facts of life, and the things they would have to expect. That year, I think they grew up a lot."

Although the Alomars went their separate ways in 1986, they stay in touch by phone.

Sandy Alomar, Sr., waves his son Roberto on to victory.

Roberto (left) and Sandy Alomar, Jr. (right), take time out with dad, Sandy Sr.

"We used to call them, and we used to tell them to call us," Sandy Sr. said. "Robbie was always calling home asking his mother how to cook certain foods, and things like that."

Sandy and Roberto's favorite dish is rice and beans. And they love chicken, too. Sandy has become an accomplished cook himself.

"We used to burn the bottom of the pan sometimes," Sandy Jr. said laughing. "But we did fine. I can cook rice, pork chops, beans, chicken. I can grill teriyaki steak, all kinds of stuff. When I was in the minor leagues, I always used to cook for my roommates."

Roberto was only seven years old when he de-

37

cided he wanted to try for a baseball career. Sandy Sr. was a switch-hitter during his own career, and taught Roberto the same skill. Even though so young, he picked up the art of switch-hitting very quickly.

"I told him it was a great advantage for him if he hit both ways," said Sandy Sr., who is now a minor league instructor and Latin Coordinator in the Chicago Cubs organization. "He didn't want to hit right-handed. He's a natural left-handed hitter. So I just kept pitching to him when I had the chance, to make him hit right-handed."

Sandy Sr.'s encouragement paid off. As a matter of fact, he says that Roberto's hitting from the right side has improved even more in the last few years. During the 1992 season, for example, he hit better from the right side than the left.

Sandy Sr. started out as a shortstop, but became a second baseman, just like Roberto is now. There's no doubt where Roberto got his hustle. Sandy Sr. is only 5 feet 9 inches tall and was not a power hitter by any means, but made up for his lack of size by playing smart baseball all the time.

Sandy Sr. is the youngest child in his own family. His brothers, Demetrio, Tony, and Rafael, each had minor league careers with the Milwaukee Braves, St. Louis Cardinals, and San Francisco Giants, respectively. All of them are quite tall and tower over Sandy Sr. It's perhaps a bit ironic that it was the little Alomar brother who went on to the big leagues. But this is not to say that the other Alomar brothers were not good players. They were. Demetrio and Tony were great fielders, and Rafael was quite a power hitter.

Since baseball is so much a part of their family, Roberto and Sandy Jr. had the chance to see the challenges and stresses of baseball firsthand. But when Roberto was asked if he'd ever thought twice about his career choice, he answered without hesitation.

"No," he said. "*Never.* I know that you go through a lot of tough times in the minor leagues. But you have to deal with it. You're going to go through a lot of good times, too."

Roberto and Sandy Jr.'s mother, Maria, wasn't always sure that their choice to become major league ballplayers was the best one, only because she knew it wouldn't be easy. She did stress that they throw themselves into their studies, too, to have something to fall back on if baseball did not work out.

"Sometimes a kid will get anything into his head," Maria Alomar said with a smile. "They saw many beautiful things. But I worried, because I know that life is not easy."

Since Sandy Sr. was away on road trips a good part of the time, Maria was often the only parent in the household. The boys also have an older sister, Sandia, who is 27 years old.

"My mom always took care of us," Roberto said. "She was a great mother. One of the reasons we are where we are is because of her. She always

39

gave us the support we needed from a mother. She is great."

The Alomar kids missed their father when he was away. But he always called from the road. Roberto says they understood that Sandy Sr. had to do his job in order to support the family. And while they didn't accompany their father on road trips, they did move to a new city each time their father went to another team. Moving can be difficult for a family. But the children enjoyed it.

"Every time my dad got traded," Sandy Jr. recalled, "I always thought it was awesome. I'd think, *We're going to see a new place!* At that time, I didn't realize it was hard. In this business, you don't have a steady home."

Even if a player remains established with one team for a long time, he still has to move year-round. Most players keep their winter homes. Then they go to their spring training site in February and, after that, they go to their major league city. And with road trips on top of *that*, it makes for a very mobile life-style.

Sandy Jr. and Roberto played ball all the time, either on the field at their father's major league or winter-ball stadium or in school and Little League. Winter ball in Puerto Rico was a bit more lenient than the majors as far as allowing players' children to run around on the field. The boys often shagged fly balls in the outfield or ran around in the bullpens during the winter months.

But another way that Sandy Jr. and Roberto honed their skills was by playing a game in Puerto

Rico called Strikeout. Someone drew a square on the wall of a building at school. This was the strike zone. According to the rules of the game, the pitcher had to strike the hitter out. Otherwise, the chances of a "base hit" were great. If the batter hit the ball and the pitcher caught it, it was an out. Of course, chances were slim that the ball would be hit right back to the pitcher. So Strikeout was a good name for the game.

"When we played two on two," Sandy Jr. explained, "it was easier. But it was fun. We used to throw hard, with rubber balls. That's the way we got used to fast pitches. We used to throw

Sandy Alomar, Jr. (left), and his brother, Roberto, look over an All-Star baseball cap.

Catcher Sandy Alomar gears up for the game.

curve balls, too, and work on our junk pitches."

When Sandy Jr. was a little boy, he began to take notice of big league catchers on television. Their heavy gear appealed to him. He was fascinated by the way the catcher would squat down, call the pitches, and see the game from that perspective. So he asked his parents for some catcher's gear of his own. One Christmas morning, seven-year-old Sandy Jr. gleefully tore open a package which revealed a catcher's mask, helmet, and pads.

But that wasn't when Sandy Jr. decided on baseball as a career. It was just fun then. During his childhood and teenage years, Sandy played some ball, rode dirt bikes, took karate and tae kwon do lessons, and even thought about becoming a pilot.

When Sandy Jr. was about 15 years old, he was going through a major dirt-bike phase. He also helped his father after school. At this time, Sandy Sr. was coaching the Puerto Rican National Team and running a gas station. One day, Sandy Jr. came by the service station, and Sandy Sr. informed him that a pony-league coach had stopped in to ask if Sandy Jr. would catch for his team in the play-offs. There were only three games left, and then the finals, and the team had no real catcher. At first, Sandy Jr. wasn't so sure.

Sandy Alomar tags out a Baltimore Oriole.

"But I gave it a try," Sandy Jr. said, "and I kind of liked it. And then, I thought, 'Hey . . . I'm *good*! I can do this!' I was a good catcher, I could hit, and I could throw well."

The team was eliminated in the finals, but an American Legion scout, who was present during the games, approached Sandy and asked him to try out for the Salinas American Legion team.

"After that," Sandy Jr. explained with a grin, "I was on a roll."

When Sandy Jr. played, word got around that the other Alomar boy had unmistakable talent, too. Scouts began to scope the field at Sandy's games. All of this attention made Sandy Jr. pretty nervous. But Sandy's father just told him to be himself, and to try and pretend nobody was there. But a man named Luis Rosa *was* there. He was a scout for the San Diego Padres who knew catching talent when he saw it. By this time, Sandy Sr. had begun coaching third base for the Padres, so the family knew Mr. Rosa. Together they worked out a contract, and Sandy Jr. was on his way.

Sandy Jr. had a challenge to meet from the start. A lot of people told Sandy Jr. that he would make the big leagues pretty fast as a catcher. But things don't always work out so neatly, no matter how much talent a player has. When he got to spring training, he was astonished to see a whole bunch of other catchers there, too. Sandy Jr. realized he had to convince everyone that he was the one good enough to make it to the majors. Benito Santiago, a well-respected and highly skilled catcher, had gotten to San Diego first. And it looked as though he was there to stay. This was rather discouraging for Sandy Jr. But then, something happened for the better. Sandy Jr. was traded to the Cleveland Indians in December of 1989. And the real Sandy became visible to all of major league baseball.

"Sandy went through a lot of tough times in the minor leagues because Benito was in front of him," Roberto said. "I'm really proud of him because he got through that quickly. And he went out there and proved that he was a great player, and that he had every reason to play in the big leagues."

Sandy Jr. is intelligent and animated, with a take-charge demeanor. He loves to talk, but he is intense and efficient behind the plate. A catcher not only needs to be strong and versatile, with good hands ready to retrieve pitches that get away, he must also be able to pick up on his pitchers' different personalities and act accordingly. Sandy demonstrated this important skill early.

He was the unanimous choice for the 1990 Rookie of the Year, and he also received a Rawlings Gold Glove award. He became the first rookie catcher to start the All-Star Game. Roberto was the National League second baseman in that game, making for a doubly special event.

Then came 1991. Baseball people often speak of the "sophomore slump," but for Sandy Jr., it was ridiculous. Altogether he missed 111 games due to injury (mainly an inflamed right rotator

Roberto Alomar leaps over a giant (a San Francisco *Giant)* *during a game.*

cuff and later a strained right hip flexor) but Sandy Jr. was determined. He would wake up at 7:00 every morning and head to the clinic for his rehabilitation. The hard work paid off. Sandy is now feeling, hitting, and throwing much better.

Sandy Jr. is one of those catchers who can zap the ball to second base to throw out a potential base stealer — from his knees. One base runner who gives Sandy that opportunity is his own younger brother. Baseball writers and fans alike enjoy watching Toronto play Cleveland. When Roberto reaches first base, everyone leans forward to see what will happen. Will Roberto try to steal? Will his brother Sandy get him out? On the field, the brothers are opponents. If Roberto bolts toward second, it's Sandy's job to whiz the ball to the bag and throw him out.

"He's doing his job and I'm doing mine," Sandy Jr. explained. "We're not going to help each other."

"We're brothers," Roberto admitted, "but we have to take care of our job. That's the way it is. If I try to steal a base, and he has to throw me out, he'll throw me out."

People all over the baseball world are whispering that Roberto Alomar may be one of the best second basemen of all time, headed for the Hall of Fame. Roberto is only 25 years old, so that's a pretty amazing compliment. He won his first Gold Glove award in 1991, and helped lead

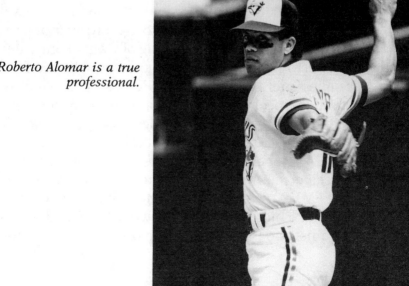

Roberto Alomar is a true professional.

his team to the American League Division Championship that same year. He stole 53 bases, second only to Rickey Henderson's 58. Twenty-one of those were steals of third base, where a player must rely on his own instinct and speed, and not the advice of a first-base coach.

"The thing that makes me most proud of Roberto is that at a young age," Sandy Jr. said, "he has accomplished things that a lot of people haven't. He's a great hitter. He's a complete player. People are saying he's the best second baseman in baseball. That makes me so proud, because his last name is Alomar. He's my *brother*. He represents me and my family, and I represent him and my family."

By the end of the 1992 season, Roberto had helped lead the Blue Jays to the American League Championship Series for the second year in a row. Their opponents were the Oakland Athletics, and Roberto had an impressive .381 batting average for the Series. One of the most-exciting moments came during the ninth inning of Game Four when Roberto hit a game-tying home run off the fearsome relief pitcher Dennis Eckersley. During the final game, the crowd stomped their feet and chanted "MVP! MVP!" in deafening tones whenever Roberto came up to bat. They got their wish. At 24, Roberto became the youngest player to receive the American League Championship Series MVP trophy. The Toronto Blue Jays went on to make history when they won the World Series against the two-time National League Champion

Atlanta Braves. They became the first non-American baseball team to capture the World Championship title.

In a game, Roberto plays second base with the self-contained assurance of a veteran. His large, intent eyes carry a solemnity that few players his age possess. He and his brother have become so well-known that it's a rare day that they aren't asked for autographs.

Sandy Sr. has taught his sons to handle the attention with grace. He tells them that the fans helped to put them where they are, so they must be accommodating. And they are. Even though sometimes, in their quest for a signature, fans might momentarily forget their manners, thrusting paper into a player's face, even if he's eating in a restaurant.

"But there's a way that you can say no in a polite way," Sandy Sr. explained. "And there's a way that you can say, 'Yes, but just give me a minute.'"

"You have to deal with being a celebrity," Roberto added. "I just try to be nice to everybody."

"It's kind of hard for baseball players to have a lot of privacy," Sandy Jr. admitted. "People just have to understand that we have our lives, too. We're human beings, like anyone else."

Maria and Sandy Sr. brought up their children very well. And it shows in their manners as well as their accomplishments. Sandia, the oldest, was never interested in the performing end of sports, but she did an excellent job in school and landed herself an impressive job. She lives in Salinas and is manager of merchandise at the Olympic Village, where the athletes train. Everyone turned out just fine. Sandy Jr.'s and Roberto's achievements just add to the family's success.

"The thing that impresses me about both of them is the respect that people have for them," Sandy Sr. said, "and the way they handle themselves as human beings. That's what makes me really proud of them."

"I feel so happy," Maria Alomar added. "See, they worked hard, and they *got* it!

4
The McRaes

When Dad's the Boss

Hal McRae grew up in Avon Park, Florida, playing stickball nearly every day as a young boy. He lived on Castle Street, which is where the stickball games were held. A rather regal name for a street, perhaps its new name is even more so to those who live in Avon Park. In January of 1992, Castle Street was renamed Hal McRae Boulevard. There was a ceremony held in Hal's honor, something he will never forget.

"That was fun," recalled Hal, a Kansas City Royals Hall of Famer and now the manager of that ball club. "I went back and saw a lot of people I hadn't seen in a long time. We would play in the road."

Hal paused for a moment, then he laughed.

"I should say the *street*," he said. "I guess it was

Hal McRae of the Cincinnati Reds jumps for joy.

a road when I grew up there. Now, it's a street! It was only a dirt road then."

Playing ball in the street rather than on an actual diamond has a different feel. Some areas were okay to hit to, while it was certainly best to avoid other places. The children tried not to play too close to parked cars — or to houses. But sometimes it was tough to avoid little misplays. For a lot of kids, baseball "accidents" are a part of growing up.

"We broke some windows," Hal admitted quickly, with a grin. "We climbed some fences. Your parents had to pay for the windows."

Obviously, no strong grudges were held against

Hal and his buddies. The people of Avon Park have every reason to feel a sense of honor that this accomplished baseball man spent his early days there. And why wouldn't they?

Hal finished his 19-year major league playing career with a .290 average and 1,097 runs batted in. He posted these numbers with the Cincinnati Reds and the Kansas City Royals. When he first came on board as the Royals manager in 1991, the Royals were the only team to improve its record following a managerial change. He replaced former Royals skipper John Wathan.

As a player, Hal was primarily an outfielder and later a designated hitter. He was an important ingredient in two National League Cham-

Kansas City Royal's center fielder Brian McRae

pionship Series and two World Series with the Reds in 1970 and 1972, back when the Cincinnati club was nicknamed The Big Red Machine. While he certainly played adeptly when called upon, Hal didn't get a lot of game time with the Reds, seeing action in an average of only 77 games per season. But once he was traded to the Kansas City Royals in 1972, things began to move along. It became pretty clear that Hal had found a niche for himself. He compiled a .293 average with Kansas City, hovering near or hitting over .300 nearly every year. In 1977, he led the American League in doubles (54) and hit .298, playing in all 162 games of the season. In 1982, he led the league with 46 doubles and 133 RBIs. He was voted onto the American League All Star Team in 1975, 1976, and 1982. So, it's pretty easy to see why Hal ranks among the top five on the all-time list in just about every Royals offensive category. And he was quite swift and smart with a glove as well.

Hal began his coaching career during his last year as a player, doubling up as a hitting coach for his teammates. After he put up the numbers he did, it's no wonder the players looked up to him as he analyzed their stances and batting techniques. He then went on to spend two seasons as a Pittsburgh Pirates minor league hitting instructor, and returned to the majors in 1990 as the Montreal Expos hitting coach. Now he's back with the Royals, a former player turned skipper.

During batting practice, Hal can be found watching his players work in the batting cage. As the batters hustle in and out of the cage to take their cuts, it may be noticed that the Royals center fielder — No. 56 — resembles the manager, right down to his batting stance. The reason is natural. His name is Brian McRae.

Brian has played sports all his life. But by the time he reached his senior year in high school, it occurred to him that he just might have a shot at making it as a professional ballplayer. When he was signed in 1985, his father was anything but shocked.

"You expected it because he was drafted number one," Hal said in a 1992 interview. "He had the full potential to play in the big leagues. This is his second year in the big leagues now, and he's done a good job. He's played outstanding center field, and he's beginning to hit some."

Brian's parents left the decision to sign a contract up to him. Even though Brian considered playing football on scholarship, he chose the baseball route. His father believes that this was the sensible choice. A football player is much more susceptible to injury than a baseball player. So Brian's athletic career could be about twice as long on the diamond as opposed to the gridiron.

Choosing baseball as a career seemed normal to Brian. In fact, since his father was a ballplayer for so long, Brian went through part of his childhood believing that everyone's parents had a job like this. After all, it was all he had known. But after a while, Brian noticed there was a difference.

"I'd go over to my friends' houses," Brian said,

"and their fathers were getting home from work. And mine wasn't. That's when it hit me that he was doing something different, and that everybody looked up to him. And they looked at *me* differently because my dad was playing ball."

By the time Brian reached the second and third grades, his classmates began to make quite a big deal out of his family situation. Often, he would be asked for autographs, both from his father and other Royal teammates. And a good part of the time, Brian was expected to provide a recap of the previous night's Royals game, complete with play-by-play analysis. His peers seemed to forget the fact that Brian was Hal's son, not the Royals general manager.

"People would ask me, 'Why did they do *this*? Why did they do *that*?'" Brian said, with a wry grin and a shrug. "And *I* didn't know! I'd think, *You watched the game just like I did!*"

The young Brian learned how to take all the attention in stride. But sometimes, it got a little tiresome. His mother, Johncyna (Jo) McRae, could — and still does — empathize with her son's feelings.

"To a kid," she explained, "it's just what your father does. It's not exciting, because it's a job."

In fact, she wasn't so sure that Brian would ever choose a baseball career after watching his father go through the same thing.

"It was so much a part of our lives," Jo explained, "and I knew other players' kids who didn't even like to come to the ballpark."

Baseball is a big part of the McRae family's life.

But she couldn't help recognize Brian's knack for sports. Jo pointed out the fact that a ballplayer's child has the opportunity to see a major league field at very close range. It becomes routine for the family that this is "just where Dad works." So baseball children become more casual about that environment than those who don't have such access to it. Perhaps this is a reason why ballplayers' kids often feel less overwhelmed when it comes to major league baseball and its players. It's a part of their everyday reality; not just a collection of baseball cards and dreams.

"Those big names are like their uncles," Jo explained. "So I think it can be a natural thing, like following your father in the business because you went to work with him all the time."

Brian has begun to make a name for himself in his first major league years. It's not unusual for him to go hurtling into the center-field wall to catch a would-be home run or spoil someone's chance of a base hit. He knows from observation and experience that the trend must always be to go forward. Hard work is part of the game, and he accepts this fact with maturity. One of the most-important lessons Hal has taught Brian is that every day, Brian must be able to say that he tried his very best.

"A lot of times," Brian explained, "you're not going to have anything. But you've got to go out there and play hard. Sometimes you're not swinging the bat well, or you're not playing good defense. If you're kind of lackadaisical, that compounds it and makes things look worse. So, you *hustle*. And if it doesn't work out, then come back the next day, and try again."

Brian observed that the game of baseball is somewhat different since the days when his father was in his heyday. For instance, today's astronomical salaries lead people to believe that baseball players can justify their incomes by playing like stars in every game. Otherwise — it might be believed — they didn't earn them.

"With the money," Brian explained, "it creates more stress. Maybe you try to do more things than you're capable of doing. If you've got a million dollar contract, you've got to show everybody that you're worth a million dollars."

58

Chances are that Brian won't have to worry about this type of criticism. He has shown that he's not afraid to go out and push himself for the good of the team. When he joined the Kansas City Royals in 1990, he finished with a .286 average. The following year — his first full major league season — Brian earned his keep. He led the club in games played (152), hits (164), triples (9), and stolen bases (20). The latter two categories illustrate his natural speed, as well as his spunk on the field. He is also the owner of the longest American League hitting streak in 1991, with 22 games from mid-July to August. He was also the Royals Player of the Month in May and August of that

Hal and Brian McRae share more than just a name.

year. And like his father, he dashed about the field impressively, making star catches all season long with only three errors.

Alike as they are, Hal and Brian don't really hang out together on the road. Part of this is simply due to their age difference and their separate sets of friends. But also, like other major league managers and sons, a professional relationship needs to be maintained. But they are able to be a family during the off-season. Hal and Jo, and Brian, are pleased that they can all spend this time together.

Brian has two younger siblings: Cullen, a 20-year-old who plays second base at Manatee Junior College in Bradenton, Florida, and 15-year-old Leah, a high school cheerleader.

"So, everybody's in the athletic mode," Hal laughed.

Only time will tell if the Kansas City Royals will win another World Championship like they did in 1985. The McRaes may well take part if it does happen. But one thing's for sure. Brian and Hal McRae have done their family — and their fans — proud.

Perhaps someday people will drive by a street sign in Bradenton, Florida, that reads Brian McRae Way. Who knows? Time will tell.

5
The Javiers

The Name — First and Last — Lives On

Julian Javier's career as a second baseman with the St. Louis Cardinals had some spectacular moments. For example, it was Julian who broke up Jim Lonborg's perfect game in the seventh inning in Game Two of the 1967 World Series, and his three-run homer helped clinch the deciding game of that Series. Julian also led the St. Louis Cardinals in stolen bases from 1960 to 1963.

During this time, one of Julian's best friends on the Cardinals was the famous slugger, Stan (The Man) Musial. Musial was one of the most-popular and effective players around.

Julian and his wife, Ynes, lived in San Francisco de Macoris in the Dominican Republic during the off-season. They already had a son named Julian Jr., who is now a cardiologist. But Julian decided that if they had another son, his name would be Stanley, after his great friend, Stan Musial.

"I told him I would use his name," Julian said of Musial, "and he said, 'Oh! Good!'"

On January 9, 1964, a baby boy was born to the Javiers. And Julian kept his word — Stanley Julian Javier was printed on the child's birth certificate. The Javiers were very happy with their new son. But little did they know that a future major-leaguer had entered the world that winter.

"I told Stan Musial one day that Stanley was going to be a ballplayer like him," Julian recalled with a smile. Musial told Julian that he hoped he was right. But at the time, they were just kidding around. Stanley was still very small.

While Stan was growing up with his older brother and three sisters — Julietta, Susy, and Linette — he became interested in all sports. Stan did admit that he wasn't that crazy about school, although he did enjoy geography.

"I liked all of the different pictures," Stan recalled, "and the class would never be the same. You always learned something new about someplace."

Stan did just fine, both in academics and with his classmates. He was well-liked among the other kids, namely because he was a good athlete. Everybody wanted Stan to be on their team.

"Every sport I played in those days, I was good at," Stan explained. "I was one of the better ones. I learned quickly. That's why my brother and I were so popular. They wanted us to play on the

The Javiers — budding baseball stars

basketball team, the baseball team, everything. Where I come from, it's a pretty large community. And we all hung around together. It's easy to be popular there."

What's not so easy is to pursue a baseball career in the shadow of your father. Stan went about it quietly. But independent as he was, it was impossible for Stan to hide his talent from his father. At first, Julian hadn't particularly followed Stan as an athlete. But someone took him aside and told him that one day, Stanley would be really good. When Julian heard that, he went to watch Stan play as soon as he could. Julian only had to see Stan play ball a few times to realize that his son was something special. But Julian kept a low profile around Stan's ballpark, because he didn't want to make his son self-conscious.

"I went to the ballpark," Julian said, "and I didn't want him to see me."

So Julian crept about quietly and observed his son's emerging talents. After getting a good look at Stan, Julian told him that he was going to bring Stan to the Cardinals spring training in St. Petersburg, Florida. Julian knew that he was more than just a proud dad. It was time for other baseball pros like himself to see his boy in action, so they planned the trip to Florida. But there was one problem. Stan was 15 years old, and he had

The St. Louis Cardinals welcome Stan Javier (center) to the team.

a test coming up in school. Julian knew how important school was, and he didn't want Stan to miss the exam. So he spoke with the school principal and explained the situation. The principal agreed to let Stan go, as long as he made up the test when he returned. Stan then impressed the Cardinals down in Florida, which led to his signing in 1981.

"And he took his test," Julian said, "and he passed the test. So, everything worked out."

Julian was excited for his son, and glad to see a possible major-league baseball career on the way. But at the same time, he couldn't help having mixed feelings. He knew that the road ahead for Stan would not be lined with roses.

"At the time," Stan said, "I didn't understand why my dad was not very happy. Now, I understand. Sometimes, you spend five or six years in the minor leagues, and you don't get anywhere. There's no guarantee when you sign a contract that you're going to make it to the big leagues."

But he did. And he has held his own. Stan, mainly an outfielder, has had the misfortune of playing for some teams with a solid outfield that was tough to crack. For example, with the Los Angeles Dodgers, he had to contend with the likes of Eric Davis, Brett Butler, and Darryl Strawberry, all everyday players. So Stan has spent some time on the bench with these teams. A lot of people might think that a player in this position has it made. He plays some games, watches some games, and gets paid all the same. But many players will say up front that it's very hard not to play every day. First of all, a player wants to be there to make a difference, to be part of the action every day. He also wants to stay sharp, mentally *and* physically, and playing every day is the way to do that. Batting and infield practice alone cannot work off the energy inside a player who wants to perform regularly. A utility player can go for days without playing an inning, yet when he's called upon, he must be ready to go at a moment's notice. This calls for a relaxed, yet conscientious, personality that can tolerate this type of pressure. Stan is an easygoing and hardworking person, so he actually fits into this category better than some other players might. But it's hard for anyone to sit and wait for a chance to play. This is something Stan is able to handle quite well, but he and his father have to talk about it sometimes.

"The hardest thing," Stan said, "is when you're not hitting. That's when somebody says, 'Do this, do that. Try this, try that.' "

When in a batting slump, a great many players turn to coaches, managers, and teammates for answers. Sometimes, it can be overwhelming, and actually counterproductive. If a slumping hitter is bombarded with suggestions, it can make him confused and much-less focused. So, many players seem to agree that the best way to handle this problem is to slow down, stop thinking so much about every little thing, and get back to basics. Just the simple things, like seeing the

Stan Javier loves being in the game.

ball, *hitting* the ball, and the like. Stanley tries to do the same thing. And Julian is always there to offer him experienced advice.

"That happened to me a lot of times," Julian pointed out. "I tell him, 'When you have a big slump, you're going to come out of it. One day, you're going to break it, and you're going to have twenty hits.' "

Julian knows how hard baseball pressures can be, especially in the minor leagues. Julian went through it in the late 1950s. Remember, major league players weren't making the kinds of salaries that are commonplace today. Minor league life is less than luxurious today, and it was much harder years ago. The wages for a minor league player were barely liveable.

"We didn't eat a lot of steak because we didn't have the kind of money to eat a big steak," Julian explained. "We would get about three or four guys from the Dominican, and we'd find some pennies and buy Milky Ways and Coke. We had to get by with that because we didn't have anything else!"

Of course, this is not a recommended diet. Their parents would not have been too happy to know that their sons were subsisting on candy and soda a lot of the time. They didn't *always* eat that badly, but they were young. And Julian and his Latin-American friends had another problem to struggle with — they didn't know English very well, only Spanish. That was fine in the Dominican Republic. But in the United States, there were not enough people who knew Spanish to help them. Day-to-day life can be difficult if you don't know the native language. So candy bars were easy to find, and it didn't take a lot of explaining to get one in a store.

"That was a long time ago," Juilian said of his early years in the game. "And it was always hard to eat because we didn't know how to order. Nobody spoke any Spanish."

After a while, the English language came a little more easily for Julian. A good way to pick up a new language is to listen. And listen. Julian decided not to tell people that he didn't know English. Instead, he listened, learned, and used a

Spanish/English dictionary until he got to the point where he did know English.

Stan found the adjustment a challenge, too. But he says he caught onto English pretty easily. In fact, many of his Latin teammates came to him for help. When a friend needed to get an apartment, Stan would speak with the real estate people for him. When someone wanted to order in a restaurant, Stan would do the talking. In addition to being a quick learner, Stan had the added advantage of knowing the United States a bit. His father, of course, had traveled all over the country. And the Javiers often vacationed in the United States.

Stan feels proud that his dad was one of the pioneer Latin-American baseball players in the United States. Now, it is common to see many Hispanic players on a major league team. But in his father's time, the notion was just beginning to catch on that there were a lot of talented baseball players south of the border.

"They opened the door for us," Stan said. "And then, the organizations started looking at the Latins more. Now, they have camps down there, and they're working hard to get players from that area."

Hitting streaks, slumps, and strange customs are all part of baseball. Being a celebrity is a significant element, too. Stan admits that he sometimes feels funny when people come up to him. He feels thankful that he often looks quite different in street clothes than in his uniform. But

Julian Javier does some fancy footwork to save the game.

still, some people figure out that it is indeed Stanley Javier walking down the street.

"You know," Stan admitted, "it comes with the territory. But I would rather that people treat me as a regular person."

But even though he feels a little embarrassed by the attention, he is always polite and cooperative.

"Sometimes I tell him, 'Don't forget to sign the autographs,' " Julian said. "Especially for little kids. They like that."

Stanley became a Philadelphia Philly on July 2, 1992. He quickly showed the Phillies that they had made the right choice. The following Sunday, he made a spectacular diving catch to rob former-

70

Dodger teammate Mike Scioscia of a base hit. So, as long as he gets the chance to play and show what he's got, he will certainly continue to maintain his celebrity status.

And his father has taught him a lot over the years, both by giving advice when needed and demonstrating his character on and off the field.

"I think that the most important thing any dad can show his kids is dedication," Stanley said. "He set a good example. I never saw him do anything wrong in my life, as a baseball player or as a father. He always emphasized that it was best to stay out of trouble. 'Stay away from people that create problems. Stay away from people who use drugs. And stay away from people who won't help you.' And that helped me. He led by example."

Now that Julian is retired, he lives in the Dominican Republic, in San Francisco de Macoris. But he is never idle.

"I've got twelve grandchildren," he boasted with a laugh, "and that makes me pretty busy."

And as long as his own children, like Stanley, continue to achieve as they do, he's going to be pretty busy for a long time to come.

6
The Stottlemyres

A Clan of Pitchers

No one can argue that Todd and Mel Stottle-myre, Jr., are not filled with great intensity. They've been that way all of their lives. The best part is that these brothers have been able to channel their energy into professional pitching careers, just like their dad, Mel Stottlemyre, Sr. Mel Sr. had a long and impressive career with the New York Yankees — inspiring his sons who came along to the ballpark to watch him pitch and to romp around the ballyard during batting practice.

As young brothers growing up together, Todd and Mel Jr.'s pep often took the form of brotherly brawls. Of course, as Todd points out, this is really the norm for two boys who are close in age — and fiercely competitive.

"We were so competitive any time we played

As youngsters, Todd and Mel Jr.'s pep often took the form of brotherly brawls.

a baseball game, a basketball game, cards, checkers, or anything," said Todd, who pitches for the 1992 World Champion Toronto Blue Jays. "If we were playing against each other, nine times out of ten, we ended up in a fight."

"We fought like cats and dogs!" Mel Jr. agreed with a laugh. Mel Jr. pitches in the Mets organization and has been rehabilitating from shoulder surgery. "We absolutely drove my mom *nuts*. But when Dad came home from a road trip, we were little angels."

One reason the young Stottlemyres shaped up a bit when Dad crossed the home threshold is easy to see. The boys just loved to go to the stadium to see their father pitch, and even practice before each game.

"We lived at the ballpark," Todd recalled. "Yankee Stadium was like a playground for us. It was a lot different back then. The kids could go to the ballpark and run around in the outfield, and hang out in the clubhouse during games. At the time, maybe we didn't realize how special we had it."

Nowadays, it's really not commonplace for the players' children to have the run of the ballpark. There would just be too many kids on the premises, and more ways to get lost, hurt, or into some kind of trouble. It takes a talented — and alert — boy or girl to be able to shag fly balls during batting practice, for example. Many organizations are staying away from this practice for common-sense reasons. It would be a shame if someone got hurt. But many major league teams have Father/Son/Daughter Days each year, giving the families a chance to be together and play a little ball game with their major league dads, complete with a play-by-play announcer on the field.

But Mel Jr. and Todd took full advantage of their privileges. And from their early childhood, they always found the time to play sports. As for the sibling rivalry, that fire has died down quite a bit. Growing out of the habit of wrangling is inevitable as time passes — even though wrangling helps *pass* the *time* when people are younger.

74

The Stottlemyres spend some time together away from the ballpark.

"We have a wonderful relationship," Mel Jr. said. "It's pretty hard for us to compete against each other right now, anyway. Todd's at the big league level where he's been successful, and I've more or less struggled to try and stay healthy. But you know, even now, we could maybe have a little competition, as far as who would get the most wins and so forth."

It's unfortunate for Mel Jr. that he has run into some bad luck in his time, having had numerous operations on his shoulder and knees. When he was attending the University of Nevada at Las Vegas, he decided to become a full-time pitcher. He had tried his hand at catching, but having to constantly squat never agreed with his knees. So, having been a pitcher much of his life anyway, he decided to take that route.

When Mel Jr. was pitching for the Kansas City Royals, he wore number 52. Everyone remembered that that was his number, since he had undergone five knee operations and two shoulder operations.

"I don't wish anybody to take the road I've taken!" Mel Jr. said with a chuckle.

Having had two rotator cuff surgeries on his right shoulder — a common injury to pitchers — Mel Jr. continued to pitch for Kansas City. A rotator cuff consists of four muscle groups located in the shoulder. When these muscles are put through too much stress, they begin to thicken. Then, as the stress continues, they begin to come apart; eventually they tear. When arm problems continued to plague Mel Jr., he had to make a decision — undergo another operation, or leave the game for good. Mel Jr. wasn't about to quit, so he had reconstructive surgery similar to that performed on Orel Hershiser of the Los Angeles Dodgers. There is a two-year recovery for this type of surgery, which entails a lot of patience and rehabilitation.

Mel Jr.'s determination is one of the many things that makes his father so proud of him. And Mel Sr. can certainly relate to his son's troubles. It was a shoulder injury that brought Mel Sr.'s pitching career to a close.

"The fact that Junior still wants to try to play major league baseball makes me feel very good,"

Mel Sr. said on a sunny mid-summer day at Shea Stadium where he is the pitching coach for the New York Mets. "I think that the majority of players, if they had to go through the things he's gone through, they would have given up. And he certainly hasn't."

"If I ever walk away from this game," Mel Jr. said firmly, "it's not going to be because I didn't work hard. Our whole family works extremely hard. That was stressed all the way through our lives, from our parents."

Mel Jr. and Sr. keep in regular touch about Jr.'s progress, especially since Mel Sr. is the coach for the major league club. Every so often, Mel Sr. receives a videotape of his son pitching in Florida at his rehabilitation assignment. Then he talks to Mel Jr. by telephone to discuss what he's seen.

In late June, when Mel Jr. spoke from his Florida training site, he talked about his progress.

"The test is going to be when I get back to the big league level and face hitters of a higher calibre," Mel Jr. explained.

It was hard for him to say when that would be, though. With an injury and subsequent operation such as his, a player needs to be monitored daily, and not be put on any timetable. But the fact that he's feeling better and "cutting it loose" when he throws the ball is a good indication that there are better days to come.

Mel Jr.'s delivery has gone through a major change. He has begun throwing from the side, not overhand like a lot of pitchers. Being a side-arm

Despite some setbacks, Mel Jr. still gives baseball his all.

pitcher is a new feeling for Mel Jr. But he is now able to get the ball over home plate *and* he says he is completely pain free when he throws in this manner. But he did admit that it felt strange at first.

Even though Mel Jr. can't actually perform in a major league game while he's in rehab, he *can* watch his younger brother take on American League hitters on television. Mel Jr. began pitching in the majors in 1990, and Todd started as a big league rookie in 1988. So they have had the opportunity to discuss hitters and how to pitch to them. Even in college, the brothers were able to compare pitching notes. They were at UNLV together for a time, and they roomed together on campus and during team road trips. That way they were able to observe each other in games, and swap bits of advice later on in their room. Both agree that when each of them is on the mound, the will to win comes tumbling out to meet opponents.

For example, both brothers are well-mannered and funny in person. But anyone can see that Todd changes when he's in a major league game. Once he steps onto the mound, he becomes a feisty, spirited hurler who puts winning above all else. His normal gentle gaze becomes a lashing stare, and when Todd's on top of his game, he can be downright intimidating.

In 1992, the Blue Jays beat the Atlanta Braves in six games in their historic World Series. Without a doubt, Todd had a hand in it. In fact, Todd didn't give up a run in the 3 ⅔ innings he pitched, and succeeded in mystifying most of the batters he faced.

Mel Jr. often displays the same intensity when he pitches.

"When we're on the mound," Mel Jr. said, "we mean business out there. We're almost too high-strung and competitive to this day. It can sometimes have a negative effect. That's something that Dad has worked on with both of us. My dad was a little more laid-back as a pitcher."

Mel Sr. has been coaching with the Mets since 1983, and had a rich pitching vocation just across town with the Yankees from 1964 to 1974. He was a strong pitcher who made the American League

All Star team five times. During three seasons — 1965, 1968, and 1969 — he won 20 or more games. Any Mets hurler, as well as each of the young Stottlemyres, knows it's a smart move to ask Mel Sr. for tips.

Mel Sr. can keep track of his sons' work from television, newspapers, or the telephone, depending upon where they are playing. When he sees that one of them might need a boost, either technically or mentally, he's ready to give them a ring.

"They know that I'm interested," Mel Sr. said, "because, number one, I'm their father, and number two, I'm involved in the game. So we have a lot in common that we can talk about."

Even though he is a great success at coaching big league pitchers, Mel Sr. also started a business back home in Washington. He opened two Stottlemyre's Athletic Stores in Sunnyside and Yakima, Washington. Yakima is home base for the family. Mel Sr. chose this line so he could deal with people who share his interest in athletic pursuits. The stores often supply young teams with sports equipment and related items. Even though it's a small business, Mel Sr. finds it very satisfying.

Todd and Mel Jr. are quick to point out that their dad and their mom, Jean, are *tops*.

"We could always be *friends*," Todd said, "and I think that was the difference. You know, they were our buddies. But at the same time, they had to lay down the law and be parents."

Jean Stottlemyre has certainly grown accus-

A classic shot! Here, Mel Stottlemyre pitches against *the New York Mets — years later he would coach them.*

tomed to being surrounded by ballplayers on all sides.

"There's no doubt she takes great pride and pleasure in seeing that my brother and I have both played pro ball," Todd said. "We had no girls in the family, so there are a lot of times when we were growing up that she was one of the guys!"

The Stottlemyres are a close, loving family that has always been able to offer support all around. Many people do not know that there was another Stottlemyre — Jason. This fun-loving brother of Todd and Mel Jr. lost his life to childhood leu-

81

The Stottlemyres have always been a close and loving family.

kemia when all three were quite young. Mel Jr.
said he believes that Todd takes Jason to the
mound with him every time he pitches. It is a
logical inspiration, because Jason showed his entire family that he was strong enough to deal with
what life dealt him. So, when times get tough,
Mel said that Todd tells him to remember how
their brother Jason lived life to the fullest while
he was here, and that they should always do the
same. The Stottlemyre family will never forget
how wonderful Jason was, and they uphold the
strength, determination, and sense of humor by
which Jason lived.

When the Stottlemyre boys were little, they

would get up early and give their weary dad a poke. He might have just gotten in late the night before from a road trip, but the boys wanted to play catch with him in the backyard. More often than not, Dad would roll out of bed and into the yard to toss the ball around with them.

"Baseball's kind of tough on families because there's so much time apart," Todd observed. "The times that you're together are the special times."

Travel is only one difficult aspect of the game. Another is being sent down to the minor leagues. A lot of players go through this, and they all agree it's *no fun*. Mel Sr. knew how to react when Todd went to the minors in 1988 and 1989. In the latter

Todd Stottlemyre fires one to the plate.

year, Todd spent six weeks with the big club. Then he was dispatched to the Triple A Syracuse Chiefs. Shocked and disappointed, he called up his father. Mel Sr. answered Todd's wails of protest with a blunt statement: "You're not there yet. You haven't even come close to reaching your capabilities."

"Those are hard words coming from your dad," Todd said. "I was looking for sympathy and he didn't have any on the other end of the line. That told me that I had a lot of work to do. I'll never forget his words."

Mel Jr. hopes one day to be coached by his dad on the big league level.

"He coached us when we were in Little League," Mel Jr. recalled. "We never lost a game. And he does a great job with the big-leaguers. He'll let a guy pitch with his own style. He doesn't try to make everybody the same type of pitcher."

Todd and Mel Jr., with their abilities and strength of character, continue to make their parents proud. For example, Todd has recorded back-to-back seasons with over 200 innings pitched and 100 strikeouts. In 1991, he led the Blue Jays staff in games started with a career-high 34. The Jays were 21–13 in games that Todd started, and his win/loss record was a more-than-respectable 15–8 with an earned run average of 3.78.

"At an early age," Mel Sr. pointed out, "I saw that they had talent, and also that they really had a great love for the game. I think that they've worked as hard as they can. That's important for anybody, to be able to look back and say, 'Well, maybe I didn't do *this*, and I didn't do *that*, but I did get everything out of my ability that I could.'"

And every Stottlemyre can say just that.

7
The Tartabulls

Upholding Excellence

When Danilo Tartabull was around 12 years old, he went up to his father, José, and told him that he would become a major league ballplayer. *And* that he would be better than José was in his own baseball career.

"And I hope *my* sons say the same thing to me," said Danny, sitting in the New York Yankees clubhouse.

Danny has a daughter, Danica, and two sons, Danny Jr. and Zachary. The boys are only six years old and nine months old, respectively, but with the Tartabull blood being what it is, who's to say that Danny's wish doesn't come true?

"Since Danny was a little kid, he always liked baseball," said José Tartabull, from his post in Davenport, Florida, where he is a minor league instructor for the Kansas City Royals.

"He always stuck around the clubhouse or was in the field, watching the players hit. And he would imitate the players a little bit, the way they swung, and stuff like that."

Danny spent many afternoons romping about Boston's Fenway Park as a child, when his father was an outfielder for the Red Sox.

When Danny began to play Little League, José sometimes watched him. That is, when he wasn't busy with his own baseball duties. José was impressed with the way Danny played the game, and also with the fact that Danny emerged as a leader among his young teammates — both on and off the field. Danny grew up in Miami, Florida, and two of his Little League teammates were Texas Ranger outfielder José Canseco and Texas Ranger first baseman, Rafael Palmeiro. All of them have Cuban ancestry as well. When they were children, though, the major leagues did not really enter their thoughts or conversations. They were just having a good time.

Danny went on to play ball in school, and his father continued to check on his progress. José proudly noted that his son had talent. Danny would hit well and run well, and he had a good, strong throwing arm.

"You know," José pointed out, "I told myself that I was sure he would play in the big leagues someday. And he's there right now!"

All one has to do is meet the Tartabulls to realize that Danny was brought up the right way. Gracious and polite, they carry themselves like

Mom Tartabull provides a great deal of support to her baseball family.

gentlemen. And on the field, they provide their teams with support and leadership.

The Tartabulls created a disciplined atmosphere for Danny, now 30, and José Jr., who is 27 and a former minor league outfielder. Their mother and father firmly set down the household laws. And they did it out of love. His mother, Maria, knew in her bones that she had a future major-leaguer in Danny. She cooked him steaks practically every day because she wanted him well-fed before ball games. She also set strict curfews for him during his high school years, and kept in regular touch with school officials to make sure Danny was getting the most out of his classes. And she never missed one of his games. To this day, Danny still calls his mother The Little General.

"She's a very, very straight, disciplinary type of person," Danny explained. "And she would always keep us in line."

About his mother, José Jr. said, "I really give her credit. As a woman, as a mother, as a friend. She really took care of Danny and spent time with him. And I respect that."

When the time came for Danny to venture out to Billings, Montana, to play his first stint of professional rookie ball for the Cincinnati Reds organization, it was an exciting time. But it was also hard for him to leave his friends and mother in Miami. José was admittedly worried about Danny, especially since he'd been through it himself.

"He started to get kind of homesick," José Sr. recalled, with an understanding chuckle. "I had to go there. I had to go to Billings and talk to him a little bit. I wanted to talk to him as a player. So, I told him, 'Danny, if you change your mind and want to come back home, it's all right with me. I'm here now, and I can take you back.'"

But the elder Tartabull had one condition: If Danny were to leave, he had to have a plan. Like going back to school and throwing himself into his studies. Danny had always enjoyed school, especially history. But now, he was playing professional baseball. And how many people get a chance to do that? He had a big decision to make — *and* a deadline. After José gave Danny his speech, he told him that he could make up his mind after the next ball game.

"So, I went to the ball game," José said. "He had a nice day that day, and hit the ball well."

The two talked things over once again. Danny told his father that he really loved the game. He had been homesick, but that would pass. Danny wanted to stay. José remained with him for about a week, and they had a good time together. Danny had made the right decision.

"And here he is!" his father exclaimed with admiration.

Sometimes, when José catches Danny on TV in a Yankee game, he'll think of something to tell him, something that might improve his game.

"We talk, and we make some suggestions," said José, "and that helps. Sometimes he agrees with me, and sometimes he doesn't."

José just wants to see Danny do well and feel good about his game. He does admit that he might be a bit tougher on Danny than he is on some of his minor league players in Florida.

"Probably because he's my son," José explained, smiling, "I act different. He says I act different with him. As an instructor with the kids, you've got to be a little bit special with them. But Danny's my *son*, you know?"

José Tartabull's lifetime batting average was a respectable .261. Not overpowering, but for a 5-foot-11-inch 165-pound ballplayer, that would be pretty difficult. More importantly, José knew how to hustle on the field, pushing his hardest to win ball games. His efforts must have helped — José was a part of the Red Sox 1967 "Impossible Dream" team. They won the American League Championship that year. And Red Sox fans and teammates remember his speed on the base paths and his genuine enthusiasm.

"When you don't hit the long ball," said José (who has two career major league home runs), "you've got to work hard to do the little things on the field. It keeps you in the game."

José grew up in Cienfuegos, a town in Cuba. When José decided to play professional ball, he left Cuba for the United States. Due to extreme

Danny Tartabull hits a three-run homer for the New York Yankees.

political unrest, he has not been able to return. It has taken a toll on him to have a relationship with his beloved Cuban relatives solely by telephone. But for him, baseball was the way to go, and overall, he is glad that he took that route.

When José arrived in the United States for his first year of pro ball, he found himself in Hastings, Nebraska. It was a long way from the town of Cienfuegos.

"Coming from Cuba," José explained, "it was hard for me. Everything was new — the language, the people, the way they live in this country, the problems with race, and stuff like that. But I had decided to be a professional baseball player, and I had heard how rough it was for some of the people from my country to get through it."

José didn't know a word of English when he arrived. It can be scary and frustrating when everywhere you turn, you hear people talking in words you don't know. José hadn't taken English in school, so he really had to start from scratch. At first, he learned to communicate with hand signals, which his manager used with him. And when people spoke, well . . . José just listened. And *listened*. Later on, he bought a Spanish/English dictionary and practiced with it every day.

"But that first year," José recalled with a laugh, "I was *blind*!"

Growing up as a Cuban-American, Danny had the advantage of learning Spanish and English. He was bilingual before he even started school. It was so natural for him to have learned both languages that he never thought about it. Today, he speaks both languages with grace and articulateness.

Danny has held onto his Cuban heritage in many ways. For instance, one of his favorite foods is *ropa vieja*, which means "old rope." *Ropa vieja* may look like "old rope," but it tastes much better! It consists of shredded beef, tomatoes, onions, peppers, and fragrant spices. It is often served with rice and beans, a Latin-American staple. He also likes *picadillo*, a delicious beef stew.

So Danny still eats well, and his performance on the field shows it. He is 6-feet-1-inch tall, weighs 210 pounds, and uses his power. He has averaged around 25 home runs over the last seven years. And it's not unusual for Danny to have 100-RBI seasons. In fact, he became the third player in Kansas City Royal history to record back-to-back 100-RBI seasons. Sluggers John Mayberry and George Brett had also performed that feat.

So there is little question why José Tartabull is so happy with Danny's career. Talent and a strong sense of family and heritage have brought the Tartabulls to where they are today.

"I'm happy that I never quit," said José with a smile. "I'm happy that I'm here in this country, and I'm happy that I'm an ex-professional ballplayer. And I'm *very* happy to have a son who plays in the major leagues right now. Thank you, God!"

8
The Alous

Like Brother, Like Father, Like Son

One of major league baseball's most exciting moments would have to be the day three brothers composed the starting outfield for the San Francisco Giants. On September 15, 1963, Felipe, Jesus, and Matty Alou took the field. But the Alou family's involvement in baseball doesn't end with these three. Today, Felipe Alou manages his son, Moises, and his nephew, Mel Rojas, in Montreal. So Expos fans now get to see the successes of the next generation.

Felipe, formerly the Expos bench coach, took over the skipper's duties on May 22, 1992, when the organization released Tom Runnells. That promotion made Felipe Alou the first major league manager to have hailed from the Dominican Republic.

Felipe is quite popular as a manager among his

The three Alou brothers take the field for the San Francisco Giants.

players, having a levelheaded and encouraging style. Because of this, it is not surprising that the Montreal Expos became serious contenders for the National League East Championship in 1992.

One thing Felipe realizes as a manager is that he has to give his players equal attention. That's one reason why, as in the case of Hal and Brian McRae, Felipe and Moises don't tend to socialize together on the road. Also, they are both very busy doing their own things.

"Moises was a little afraid for maybe a player to see us together too much," Felipe explained. "That's the way I feel. We just don't want anybody to say, 'Hey, that's the manager's boy,' or whatever. But I'm pretty sure that the players understand."

Now that Moises is an Expo, Felipe can observe his accomplishments firsthand. As his *father*, Felipe can't help but be filled with pride. But technically, Moises is just another player on his roster. During the game, he instructs all of the players in a consistent way, showing no favoritism. There is just no placc for that on the field. And the Alous understand that perfectly. All the same, Felipe is quick to say that he always knew that Moises would enter the field of professional baseball and that he would do well.

"I expected it," Felipe said quickly. "Yes, very much. He has all of the ingredients, not only to be a good athlete, but to be a major-leaguer. He has every one of them — dedication, toughness, intelligence. I could see all of that when he was growing up."

Felipe said that he didn't even feel too worried for his young son when Moises first began his minor league trek toward the majors. He knew that Moises had the tools to deal with it.

"I saw the calibre of people who are in the big leagues," Felipe said, "and I thought he could be one of them. I thought, 'Gee, my kid is as good as some of these people.' I was afraid for his career when he hurt his right shoulder and had to go through a major operation. But thank God, he's back. That tells me I was right when I thought I had a really tough son."

Moises made it through 1991 in one piece. But it was as far from ideal as it could be for a major league ballplayer who had paid his dues and made it to "The Show." That year, he was unable to play a game. During the first part of the off-season, Moises began playing winter ball at Escogido, in the Dominican Republic. On November 28, 1990, Moises accidently slammed his right shoulder. He had been on first base trying to avoid a pickoff attempt. As he dove back to the bag, he landed awkwardly on his shoulder.

By the time spring training rolled around, he felt more or less ready to play again, even though he was aware of some pain. Moises didn't want that to stop him. If possible, he would play through the discomfort without making an issue of it. It was his first chance to start the season with a big league team, and he didn't want to be stopped in any way from helping the Expos.

Moises played in some exhibition games in West Palm Beach, where the Expos train, as well as around Florida's Grapefruit League. But by March 19, even though he had been able to swing the bat with some proficiency, he had to admit that something was indeed wrong with his shoulder. That day he was placed on the disabled list. It was a safe, smart move on the Expos' part, especially since Moises hadn't been healthy enough to play the outfield.

A shoulder operation was scheduled for April 10, 1991. Moises had two major tears in the shoulder, including a rotator cuff injury, like Mel Stot-

Montreal Expos coach Felipe Alou

tlemyre, Jr. Once the surgery was performed, Moises began a serious training and rehabilitation program. He still traveled with the Expos, but he had no job with them as a player that year. He couldn't bear not to be helping the team in some way, so he kept busy by operating the radar gun in the stands behind home plate to keep track of how fast the pitchers threw. It was better than *nothing*. But it wasn't exactly the position Moises had counted on having for the 1991 season.

Moises didn't play ball until the following winter. He played again in the Dominican Republic, for the Aguilas team. It's a safe bet that Moises thought twice before he hastily dove into any more bases. He'd come so far, and the only direction Moises want to go in was forward.

And he's done that! In 1992, Moises came back from his injury. The Expos weren't sure how often Moises would play, but he did quite well and ended up in more than a few games. His chance had finally come — he could go out there and show his team what he had.

"He's done some things that players don't usually do after missing a twelve-month period like he did," Felipe pointed out.

When the Expos everyday left fielder, Ivan Calderon, went down with an injury, Moises began to play left field more often. It was an adjustment for him, since he had primarily been a center fielder. But Moises did the job dutifully, making some good plays and getting some impressive hits in Calderon's absence.

"All of those things are signs to me that we have a pretty good ballplayer here," Felipe said.

Moises was 18 years old when he committed to a baseball career. He was first signed on by the Pittsburgh Pirates in January, 1986.

When he and his cousin, Mel Rojas, were young, they were among the many children who played impromptu baseball games in the streets of the Dominican Republic. Meanwhile, Moises' dad, Felipe, and his uncles, Jesus and Matty, were making quite a name for themselves playing baseball in the United States. But during winter-ball games, Felipe had a chance to spend time with his son. He saw that Moises was an aggressive and confident youngster as he raced about the outfield in his small uniform, shagging fly balls.

Moises didn't actually play organized baseball until he went to college. He attended Cañada College in Redwood City, California, for two years. He was sent to college on a scholarship set up by San José stockbroker Don Odderman. In 1985, Moises attended classes and hit .340 for the Cañada baseball team. The next year he led his league with an average of .447, including nine home runs. Pretty soon, scouts were whispering about the Alou boy in California. It seemed that he was ready to sign a pro contract with some organization. Moises thought it would be a good idea, too.

"I talked to my dad," Moises said, "and he wanted me to go to school for like, two more years. But he left it up to me. He told me, 'This is what I want you to do. But if you want to sign, go ahead and sign.'"

So, after much thought, Moises accepted the offer to play ball for the Pirates organization.

It's obvious that the Alou family is very involved and extended.

"We are a large family," Moises said, when asked to count all of his siblings. "I have three younger brothers. They're back home in the Dominican Republic. And I've got three younger sisters who live in Atlanta. My older sister is Maria, then comes José, then me."

Felipe and Maria, Moises' mother, have three children: José Moises, Maria, and José. Felipe has since remarried and has several daughters. Six-

Moises Alou showed talent at a very early age.

year-old Valerie is trilingual, speaking English, Spanish, and French.

"She's really something!" Felipe said with a smile.

There are also a number of young sons in the Alou family.

"A lot of players coming up!" Felipe laughed.

Moises' sister, Maria, is now married, but she played basketball as a student at Arizona State University. José played baseball in the Expos farm system, but a serious shoulder separation cut his career short. José actually played minor league ball under his father's management in Florida.

"But he started too late," Felipe explained,

101

"and then he couldn't play anymore. He was hitting .333 and playing every day for me."

The Alous don't have just baseball in common. They also all know what it's like to travel to another country for their employment. It can be pretty overwhelming for anyone starting a new job, especially if they have to move away from home — *and* learn a new language on top of that.

"Everything was different," Felipe said. "The culture, the language, the food, the nationality difference. Coming from a very very poor, underdeveloped country to one of the richest developed societies in the world — that was a big adjustment. My brother Matty was only seventeen when he got here, and Jay (Jesus) was sixteen. So, that was really a shock to those guys."

Jesus admitted to feeling quite lonely when he first got to the United States. But he also pointed out that, since he was only 16 years old, he wasn't really aware of how difficult his situation was. He found it exciting, too. But he does remember an important conversation he had with one of his brothers. When he and Matty were on the plane together heading for the United States, Matty told Jesus something he would never forget.

"You are black," Jesus recalls Matty saying, "and there is a difference between black and white in the country we are going to. So, don't ever forget that you are black."

"Before then," Jesus explained with a surprised little laugh, "I really didn't know what I was! It made no difference to me."

Racism and prejudice is something that everyone has to deal with on some level. But Jesus said that his situation really wasn't too bad for him. One likes to think that race relations in the world are steadily changing for the better — however slowly. Jesus said that the Santo Domingo area, where he grew up in the Dominican Republic, is changing, too.

"When we were little," Jesus said, "we had no electricity. And there were a lot of fish out in the ocean. We were out in the country, you know? And now, there is electricity, and no fish in the ocean. It is the city now.

"But the weather is the same," Jesus went on. "It's tropical. There are a lot of thunderstorms during the summer, and a very nice, cool breeze from the north in winter. And there is a lot of fruit, mangoes and stuff, growing all over the place."

Jesus is now a scout for the Expos. In fact, he signed his nephew, pitcher Mel Rojas.

"It was hard," said Mel, when speaking about his own adjustment to the United States once he signed. "You've got to play hard and work hard. And only worry about baseball. That's where your mind should be, on the field."

In 37 appearances with the Expos, Mel compiled a 1991 record of 3 wins and 3 losses, with a 3.75 earned run average and 6 saves. He came in third in the Expos Player of the Month voting in September and October, when he had an excellent 1.00 ERA with 2 wins, no losses, and 4

Pitcher Mel Rojas was signed to the Montreal Expos by his uncle Jesus Alou.

saves. That same year, he had 4 wins and 2 losses with a 4.10 ERA with the Indianapolis Indians, the club's Triple A affiliate. But when he was with Montreal, he showed everyone that he was a pitcher of major league quality.

When Moises was starting out in pro ball, he had the advantage of knowing some English. He had been to the United States before. And going to college in California helped him a great deal.

"I took English in high school," Moises said. "But some guys, when they come here, they don't know anything. I think it's very tough for the Dominican player, or the Puerto Rican player — whatever — to come to the States when they first sign."

But it was tough for Moises when he first arrived in California for college.

"I was very homesick my first two weeks," Moises recalled. "I mean, that was the first time I left home on my own. But after that, I made some friends. It took me like, three weeks to get used to it. I started to learn the language a little better. Once I got better in English, everything was okay."

Latin-American people eat a lot of rice and beans. In fact, Moises' favorite food is rice and beans. He also likes chicken, especially the way his mom makes it.

"It's like broiled chicken," Moises explained. "She puts tomato sauce on it, and oil."

Felipe was surprised to see the amount of steak that Americans eat when he first came to the United States. The meat that he and his family ate back home was stew beef.

"It took me about three years to find out that Americans also eat stew beef," Felipe said. "I hadn't known enough English to order it. And I didn't see a lot of rice. Over there, we eat rice every day. It's almost like a rule. It's just custom. That's the way it is. We got it from Spain. The Spanish eat a lot of rice."

Like a lot of Latin people, Felipe enjoys eating fried plantains. Plantains are a form of cooking banana. They can be sliced and fried when they are still green, and they then resemble large, slightly soft potato chips. When plantains ripen and become yellow, they can also be fried. Then they are often sliced more thickly, and taste sweet.

"I eat a lot [of plantains]," Felipe said, "every day. Green and yellow, for either dinner or lunch. That is pretty good, too."

Moises also spends a lot of time listening to the music of his culture. His favorite band is La Coco Band, which plays merengue music. He also plays the guiro, which is used in merengue music. It is a long instrument made of aluminum, with many holes. When played, it makes a *ch'k'ch'k'ch'k'ch'k* sound in the background of a song.

Moises also enjoys basketball, fishing, and snorkeling. But like many of his relatives, he certainly keeps himself busy with baseball.

So, when is the Alou legend going to end? With all of these family members involved in the game, it doesn't look as though it's going to end any time soon. And chances are great that no one is too disappointed.

9
The Boones

A Three-Generation Miracle

On Wednesday, August 19, 1992, the Boone family made baseball history. That was the day that 23-year-old Bret Boone made his major league debut with the Seattle Mariners. In doing so, the Boones became the first baseball family to have three generations play in the majors. Bret, a second baseman, has proven himself, as his father, Bob, and his grandfather, Ray, have. It was inevitable that the possibility would become a reality.

"He'll definitely play in the big leagues," said Bob Boone in a telephone interview three weeks before his son's debut. "It's just a matter of time, and it's a matter of if he can. I mean, he's certainly got the tools to be there and to stay there. But all of that is going to be on him. You never know how people will react once they get there."

107

*Father and son, Bob and
Bret Boone, practice
batting.*

It seems that Bret has reacted just fine. After
less than three seasons in the minor leagues, Bret
received word that he was about to become a big-
leaguer. It was time to make history.

"It was the third inning of my game down in
Calgary," said Bret, recalling his call-up. "And
we came off the field. And the skipper [Keith
Bodie] came up to me and said, 'Hey, you're
going. Congratulations.' At first, I was kind of in
a daze. It was a great feeling. I was excited. The
only thing is, I had to sit around and watch the
rest of the game. And it was an extra-inning game
and I was there for about three hours after they
told me. So, I was kind of antsy and ready to go.
But it was definitely a thrill."

Naturally, he called his father and grandfather to tell them his exciting news.

"But they already knew," he said with a grin. "They had heard before I heard. I think they were excited. I could tell just by talking to them that they were. I mean, they are not the type to get excited really *easily*. But I could tell just by the tone of their voices that they were excited."

Of course, the story didn't end there. The Saturday after his call-up, Bret hit his first major league home run off Boston right-hander (and, strangely enough, former Seattle Mariner) Mike Gardiner.

"Oh, that was great," Bret said, his eyes sparkling with enthusiasm. "To get it in Fenway Park, such an historic place, was exciting. When I hit it, I knew it was out. And I just wanted to get around those bases and get into the dugout. It was definitely a thrill for me."

To say the least, it was pretty interesting for him to grow up in a family that was so established in baseball. "My grandfather was probably the first person to put a ball and a bat in my hands," said Bret. "I think he was a major influence early in my life."

"Having him as a grandson is exciting to me and to his grandmother," said Ray Boone, now a scout for the Boston Red Sox in the San Diego area. "He's pretty special. Bob had Bret at an early age, and when Bob went into the service, I had Bret a lot during those six months. We've become very close."

The first player in the clan, Ray was a major-leaguer from 1948 to 1960. He started his pro career as a catcher. Later, he moved to the infield, playing shortstop, then third and first base.

"When I was a catcher," Ray explained, "it was just part of growing up as a kid. In my neighborhood, I was always the catcher."

But shortly after he entered the field as a professional, he was asked by his manager to give shortstop a try.

"That was kind of a tough assignment," Ray said. "The only thing I regretted about the move was the fact that I hadn't played the infield as a kid. But the whole thing turned my career around. I was always a skinny kid. And once I stopped catching, I started to mature and put on weight. And I got much stronger."

That he did. Ray went on to the major leagues and stayed there for 13 years. When he finished with the Boston Red Sox, he had accumulated a very respectable .275 batting average. He hit 151 home runs, eight of which were grand slams. Going from catcher to infielder worked out well for him, because he found that he was pretty good around the bag. He was an All-Star third baseman with the Detroit Tigers. And he was a very hard worker. That is something that his son Bob learned and inherited, too, as well as Bret.

Bob and his brother, Rod, used to accompany Ray to the ballpark as children. Rod and Bob grew up and formed the Boone Construction

Company in Orange County, California. They have a sister, Terry, who is an interior designer in Minneapolis. But when the boys were young, baseball was a key pastime for them. Ray looked at his son Bob and figured that he would probably be a ballplayer as an adult. When it actually happened, Ray took it in stride.

"I thought he would be a major league ballplayer," said Ray, "just like I thought from day one that my grandson, Bret, was going to be a major leaguer. We never talked about it. You could tell from the get-go that it was something Bob would pursue. Baseball was his life."

Bob has some vivid memories of what it was like to go to work with Dad as a small child.

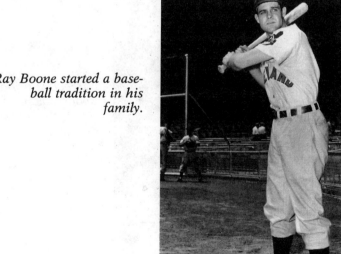

Ray Boone started a baseball tradition in his family.

"When I was *really* young, probably two or three," said Bob, now the manager for the Tacoma Tigers, the Oakland A's Triple A club, "my dad played with the Cleveland Indians. I can remember things about Cleveland. I remember driving over bricks going to the ballpark. In Detroit, I remember the smell of the hot dogs. I was looking for vendors all the time."

When Ray went on to play for the Chicago White Sox, children of the players were allowed to work out on the field.

"Then, I went to the ballpark every second!" Bob said. "I wore Nellie Fox's uniform. He was the great second baseman. I wore his uniform

Baseball is in Bob Boone's blood.

because he was the smallest guy on the team, and *I* was small."

Strangely enough, Bob started out as a third baseman when he signed with the Philadelphia Phillies. Then, he switched from third baseman to catcher, kind of the reverse of what his father did. Bob was a pitcher and third baseman all through Stanford University, where he received a degree in psychology. When the famous infielder Mike Schmidt arrived at the Philadelphia playing field, he was a shortstop. But management decided that Mike would make a great third baseman. They certainly turned out to be right. Bob had been at third base, and he was pushed 90 feet down the foul line to home plate and received some catcher's gear. And shortly thereafter, everyone saw one of the best catchers in the game emerge.

"It was the greatest thing that ever happened to me," Bob said. "When I was asked to do it, I was very leary. But I always felt that my amount of range at third base would force me into catching. Even when I was in college, I had always felt in the back of my mind that I would be a catcher. I had all of the attributes: really good hands and a good throwing arm. And I was really fast — for about two feet! Then after two feet, I was very slow. And that's how catchers are built."

Bob certainly proved that catching was his niche. During his major league career, Bob won seven Rawlings Gold Glove awards. He won his first Gold Glove in 1978, which snapped the 10-year winning streak of the great Cincinnati Reds catcher, Johnny Bench. He has been in four All-Star games (1976, 1978, 1979, and 1983). He and Ray are the second father/son combination in major league history to each record 100 or more home runs. Ray had a total of 151 and Bob hit 105. (Gus and Buddy Bell were the first, in 1979.) His best year for batting average was 1988 when he was with the California Angels and hit .295 with five homers. He holds major league records for games caught (2,225) and the most years with 100 or more games caught (15). In 1987, he caught in 63 consecutive games from July 27 to October 4, a difficult feat to accomplish, since catching takes its toll on the body. He has taken part in six league-championship series, and was involved in the 1980 World Series when he played for the Phillies.

So, in the same way that Ray was an inspiration to *his* children, Bob and Ray were inspirations to Bob's children. Bob has two other sons, Aaron, 20, and Matthew, 14. Aaron, a sophomore at the University of Southern California (where Bret also attended), is currently tearing up the baseball turf and is already impressing scouts.

"He was drafted out of high school by the [California] Angels," explained Bob. "He elected to go to USC, and he won't be eligible for the draft now until after his junior year."

Both of the older boys showed early on that

their interest in baseball wasn't just a passing thing.

"Bret was playing on three teams during the summer," Bob said. "He never had to make the statement, because it was pretty obvious. It was fairly obvious with all of the kids from the time they were a year old. It was the same with myself and my dad. I knew what I wanted to do from the time I was one or two years old."

Bret and Aaron went to the ballpark with their father constantly, including the Father/Son games. The Philadelphia Phillies were another club that allowed players' kids to come to the ballpark and play in the field. Not all teams were

Bret Boone covers second base.

willing to do that, and Bob is especially thankful that the Phillies let his sons come to the park with him.

"I really have a soft spot in my heart for the Phillies for allowing that," Bob said. "It's a unique situation, where kids can go to the office with Dad every day. That's kind of unheard of. As a father, this game is a killer, being a family person. You play a big part of the game for two to three months when the kids are in school. And you've got the swing shift. So you're not getting to bed until two o'clock in the morning, which means that you have to sleep in. And your kids are on the day shift. So you sleep in, the kids go

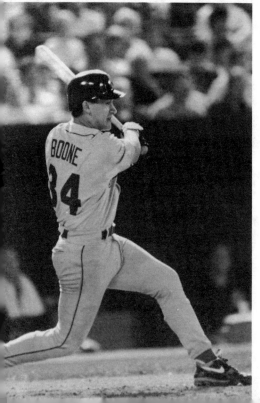

Like his father and grand-father, Bret Boone knows what to do at the plate.

to school, and then you leave for the park just before they get home. So even though you're home, you may never see your kids!"

Bret just loved to go to the stadium and shag balls with the major-leaguers.

"It was fun growing up in that atmosphere," Bret said. "At the time, I don't think we realized how lucky we really were. But I look back on it, and those were some of the best times, being able to suit up and be one of the guys."

And now, Bret *is* one of the guys. But it didn't happen automatically. Bret had to put in the time. From the moment he put on a professional uniform, he started to work. He knew that was the only way he would make it.

Ray and Bob understand about hard work. After all, they both did it themselves. With their current jobs, they are constantly exposed to young players. Ray sees kids trying to sign with a pro ball team, and Bob has to manage the Triple A players in Tacoma, all of whom are working hard trying to get over that last hurdle and into the majors.

"There are things [Bret's] worked on as a minor league player," Bob explained, "like cutting down on strikeouts and chasing pitches. But he has to maintain his aggressiveness. One of his real plusses is that he's extremely aggressive with the bat. But with aggressiveness comes strikeouts. So, he's working on that. That comes with experience. And he works a lot on turning double plays. It's really all aspects of the game, trying

117

to improve on them and develop. And that's what being in the minor leagues is all about, for everybody."

There is a fine line between being aggressive at the plate and being too cautious. Obviously, it would not be smart to stand in the batter's box and let perfectly hittable pitches sail by. On the other hand, it's not a good idea to swing at every pitch that comes somewhere near home plate. In other words, a player needs to learn how to be patient and wait for his pitch. But he can't spend the whole time waiting either, or he might miss his chance.

"I've told a lot of kids, 'Boy, you've got to be aggressive!' " Ray said. "And now, we get somebody who's aggressive, and you've got to say, 'Hey, calm down!' But my idea of the whole thing is this: If you're producing and putting up decent numbers, well, don't change. There's an old saying, 'Don't fix it if it's running.' "

It's a very good saying indeed. And it's fitting if it's a favorite expression of Ray Boone's. After all, it's a motto by which the entire Boone family should — and does — live. The three-generation miracle has finally happened in baseball. And there are probably a few more miracles down the road.

10
More Baseball Brothers

Say Brother!

The list of baseball families is practically end-less. After all, there have been over three hundred sets of brothers in the big leagues!

Harold Reynolds, born in Eugene, Oregon, is a popular second baseman with the Seattle Mariners. People may not know that two of his brothers, Don and Larry, played professional baseball, mostly in the minor leagues. Don played outfield in the majors for the San Diego Padres, and later played and coached in the Mariners system. Larry played in the Texas Rangers and St. Louis Cardinals organizations.

Now Larry is one of Harold's agents, and Don is a coach for the Houston Astros. When they were little, the Reynolds brothers spent a lot of time playing ball.

"They taught me a lot," recalled Harold, who

Don Reynolds played out-field for the San Diego Padres.

comes from a family of eight children. "My main job was to shag balls while they hit. I'm the youngest in the family, so I think I benefited more than they did."

Harold's mom, Lettie, had a pretty big job, raising eight children. The house was always filled with people. The Reynolds family has remained quite close. As a matter of fact, they all spent Christmas 1992 at Disney World in Florida.

Harold responsibly grasps his celebrity status by being extremely active in civic and humanitarian efforts in his community. There's no doubt he's made his mother and family very proud.

"It wasn't like she was raising these kids to be major league baseball players," Harold explained. "We all wanted to go to college, and then, it was just like the next step. I'm sure now my mom is a little more aware and appreciative of the sport. I think she learned with each one of us. She gets to travel and watch me play quite a bit."

George and Ken Brett are another brother tandem in the majors. George is the star third baseman/first baseman/DH for the Kansas City Royals. George has won the Royals Player of the Year seven times. The 13-time All-Star has led the Royals in many categories, including games played, hits, doubles, home runs, RBIs, walks, and batting average. He was the proud owner of a 30-game hitting streak in 1980. It's pretty ob-

Harold Reynolds is a popular second baseman with the Seattle Mariners.

Ken Brett claims there was no competition between him and his brother George.

vious why George is a favorite among Royals fans.

George was able to learn a bit about baseball by watching his brother Ken go through it first. Ken is four-and-a-half years older than George.

"George asked me questions and we talked about baseball after I signed my contract," said Ken, a major league journeyman pitcher for 14 seasons. "I signed my first contract with the Red Sox, and left home pretty much for good. George was just graduating from Little League. Quite honestly, there was no competition between George and me because I was always bigger and stronger than he was."

Now, while George plays for the Royals, Ken broadcasts games for the California Angels. There are four Brett brothers altogether. John is a building contractor. Bobby runs two minor league baseball teams, Spokane, Washington, in the Northwest League and Riverside in the California League. The family also owns a minor league hockey team in Spokane. Talk about a family with ambition!

Tony and Chris Gwynn grew up in Los Angeles, California. It became clear early on that baseball was their game.

"We played every day in the backyard," re-

Chris and Tony Gwynn always knew baseball was their game.

called Chris, who plays outfield for the Kansas City Royals. "We had a lot of fun during the summer months. As long as we had a bat and a ball in our hands, we were happy."

And such is the case today. Tony is a four-time batting champion with the San Diego Padres. He's an outfielder, too.

Like the Brett brothers, the two Gwynns are four years apart. So they did not compete together on an organized team. But Tony was still happy to offer Chris advice whenever he looked for it. Tony would show Chris certain baseball techniques, adding that Chris could apply his knowledge when his time came to play as a pro.

Chris was smart to listen to his big brother. Tony has five Gold Glove awards and makes the All-Star team practically every year. In 1991, Tony committed only three errors and led the team with eight outfield assists. Tony is a club leader for the San Diego Padres in batting, hits, runs, doubles, triples, stolen bases, and games played. (Sounds a lot like George Brett, doesn't it?) Both played exemplary baseball, much to the pride of their respective ball clubs.

Chris was quick to explain that whenever he and Tony catch up with each other on the telephone they talk about "everything but baseball." There's a lot more to their lives, even though the sport is a big part of each of them.

"We ask, 'How's the family? How are the kids?'" said Chris.

Steve Sax plays second base for the Chicago White Sox.

There is another sports-minded family from the Sacramento, California, area. Steve and Dave Sax used to play games constantly when they were kids. Steve plays second base for the Chicago White Sox, and Dave was a catcher in the New York Yankees system. There was never any doubt in the Saxes' minds that their two boys would someday play ball for a living.

"They knew ever since we were little kids what we wanted to do," said Steve. "They always gave us the opportunity to go practice and play."

The Sax brothers played organized baseball, but they also competed against each other in their backyard. They used a tennis ball and pitched to each other.

125

Dave Sax was a catcher in the New York Yankees system.

"If a ground ball passed you," Steve explained, "in between the fence and the tree, it was a double; in between the tree and the street, it was a triple; and if you hit it in the street, it was a home run."

A lot of kids use the environment that they're in to work on their sports skills. A real baseball diamond isn't always necessary. This particular game paid off for the Sax brothers.

Steve and Dave have three sisters: Cheryl, Dana, and Tammy. Tammy used to join her brothers a lot when they played in the yard.

"She's a really good athlete," Steve said, "an outstanding softball player. In fact, she still plays once in a while on teams. She's tall, and she's got a good, athletic body."

One Christmas, Mr. and Mrs. Sax bought young Dave and Steve football equipment, complete with plastic helmets and pads.

"And they got Tammy the same thing," Steve said. "She played football with us, and basketball and baseball."

The Sax children all stay in touch with each other. Steve and Dave talk on the phone, comparing baseball notes.

"We talk about other things, too," said Steve, who is the younger of the two brothers. "My brother and I are very close. We share everything, really."

And all of these brothers share the special baseball talents that got them to the big leagues.

11
Historical Chapter

Some Names from the Past

Just about everyone has heard of the famous New York Yankees outfielder/slugger Joe Di-Maggio. This Californian, whom many people called Joltin' Joe, had a magnificent major league career from 1936 to 1951. In his first big league season, he led the league with 15 triples. The very next year, he scored a league-leading 151 runs and hit an incredible 46 home runs. Eleven years later, in 1948, he hit 39 home runs. All in all, Joltin' Joe averaged about 28 home runs per season. And he was no slouch with a glove.

But he also wasn't alone in his accomplishments.

Joe's younger brother Dom was tearing up the turf for the Yankees rival, the Boston Red Sox, from 1940 to 1953. Not quite the power hitter that Joe was, Dom could still help the Red Sox

The DiMaggio brothers — Vince, Joe, and Dom — take the field again.

just fine — both in the outfield and by hitting for average. In 1950, Dom hit 11 triples, more than anyone else in the league. (Joe came close, hitting 10 that year.) Dom finished his career with a .298 batting average. Dom's nickname was The Little Professor, since he looked so collegiate in his eyeglasses and only stood 5-feet-9-inches tall.

But the DiMaggio story doesn't end there. They had an older brother, Vince, who spent his big league career playing for the Boston Braves, Cincinnati Reds, Pittsburgh Pirates, Philadelphia Phillies, and New York Mets. His best year was 1941 with the Pirates, when he hit a more-than-respectable 21 home runs and drove in 100 runs.

In 1945, four of his 19 homers for the Phillies were grand slams.

There is another, more-recent story about three historic baseball brothers. Many people recall the famous game when the three Alou brothers formed the San Francisco Giants outfield for an inning. The date was September 15, 1963. Felipe played right field, Matty manned center field, and Jesus played in left.

"We're very proud of it," Felipe said. "Because this is history that we are talking about. It hasn't been accomplished since. But I believe we feel prouder now, after we've gotten older. At that time, we didn't know it was that big."

"That was no different for me," pointed out Matty, "because we had already played a lot of baseball together."

In the Dominican Republic, where the brothers grew up, they often took up the outfield together in winter ball. Matty said that they all played together for about eight years. So, it really wasn't a shock for them.

The Alous got their early training by playing improvisational baseball in their yard. They didn't set up a diamond. Being quite poor, they didn't have ideal equipment, to say the least.

"We used sticks," Jesus explained, "rubber balls, bottle caps, and whatever we had. Hitting was our thing. Baseball, if you could call what we played baseball, meant to hit something, to make contact."

The Alous will go down in history. There are literally hundreds of brother combinations in the major leagues, and over a hundred father/son players. Many of the more famous baseball families are brothers.

Henry (Hank) Aaron's career lasted from 1954 to 1976 with the Milwaukee and Atlanta Braves, then later with the Milwaukee Brewers. Virtually every year, Hank led his league in at least one offensive category. He ended his career with a .305 batting average. His younger brother, the late Tommie Aaron, played with Hank from 1962 to 1971.

Three brothers who came from Arroyo, Puerto Rico, played together for the St. Louis Cardinals in 1973. They are José, Hector, and Tommy Cruz. Later on, they went their separate ways, to different teams. Of the three, José had the longest major league career — 19 years.

People may recall the antics and enthusiasm of Dizzy Dean, a star pitcher who played from 1930 to 1947 for the St. Louis Cardinals and Chicago Cubs. His brother, Paul, was also a pitcher, and shared the St. Louis uniform with Dizzy for four years. In 1934, the Dean brothers combined for an amazing 49 wins during the regular season. The following year, they won 47 together.

The Niekro brothers, Phil and Joe, are another

Paul and Dizzy Dean caused a sensation in their time.

colorful pitcher combination. Both pitched for various teams from the late 1960s to the late 1980s. Phil was mostly famous for pitching in Atlanta, and Joe spent much of his career with the Houston Astros.

Gaylord Perry was a notorious pitcher from 1962 to 1983. His brother, Jim, also pitched from 1959 to 1975.

Boston Red Sox fans will always remember the late Tony C. Tony Conigliaro was a great outfielder for Boston, and his younger brother, Billy, joined him there in 1969 and 1970. Tony's career was cut short when he was hit by a pitch in the left temple. He made a valiant attempt at a comeback, but was never the same again. But the fans who watched him will never forget Tony C. Today, Boston's Jack Clark wears No. 25 in honor of Tony, who wore that number during his Boston years. His legend lives on.

As for fathers and sons in baseball history, Yogi Berra and his son, Dale, make a memorable pair. Yogi was a catcher for the Yankees, and Dale spent most of his career as an infielder with the Pittsburgh Pirates. Yogi even managed Dale for a time, the way Cal Ripken, Sr., managed his sons.

Yogi Berra gives some advice to his son, Dale.

Connie Mack was one of the most-famous early ballplayers. He played from 1886 to 1896. He had a son, Earle, who played in the majors from 1910 to 1914.

Paul (another person nicknamed Dizzy) Trout pitched from 1939 to the 1950s, mainly for Detroit. And his son, Steve, played from the late 1970s to the late 1980s for Chicago (both the White Sox and the Cubs), the New York Yankees, and the Seattle Mariners.

Of course, there are a great many more fathers, sons, and brothers in baseball history. There are almost too many to name. And who knows how many more will be added to the list in the years ahead?

12
Nolan and Reid Ryan

A Game to Remember

Nolan Ryan, the high-kicking, fireballing pitcher for the Texas Rangers, has been in the major leagues since the late 1960s. He brings a lot of excitement into a ball game — for fans, teammates, and opponents alike.

Nolan, his wife, Ruth, and their three children have been around sports all their lives. It's not at all surprising that the kin of Nolan Ryan are greatly enthused by pursuits of all kinds.

"Ruth was a state champion in tennis in high school," Nolan said of his wife. "She's very athletic. Growing up in Texas when she did, girls didn't get to participate in much. There was just volleyball and tennis, really. So, she was a tennis player."

Now that Ruth Ryan has spent a lot of time in the baseball world, she has played on several soft-

Nolan Ryan pitches to his son Reid, an up-and-coming major-leaguer.

ball teams and is able to coach the children. In fact, she went to the Texas Rangers Fantasy Baseball Camp during the winter of 1992. Fantasy Camp gives adult fans the chance to dress in big league uniforms and play the game every day for two weeks. Major league heroes are on hand to give the campers expert advice. Ruth enjoyed it very much and, not surprisingly, she did very well.

The Ryan kids are Robert Reid, Nolan Reese, and Wendy Lynn. Seventeen-year-old Reese is active in both baseball and basketball, and 16-year-old Wendy plays basketball and volleyball. Twenty-two-year-old Reid has turned his focus to baseball. Reid is a junior at Texas Christian University in Fort Worth, Texas, and he pitches for the baseball team.

"I think I'm very fortunate that my kids are all athletic and like sports," said Nolan. "They have a lot of interest in baseball. They enjoy being around it. And I spend a lot of time at the gym or ball field watching them. So it's a real family thing for us."

While Reid is in school, he plays against teams at his own collegiate level. But when Reid was a freshman at the University of Texas, his baseball team — the Texas Longhorns — played a special exhibition game against some players from the Texas Rangers, including his own father, Nolan. Not everyone gets to play a serious game against a relative. The fact that Reid's father is an accomplished major-leaguer made this game all the more exciting and special. This competition took place on April 2, 1991, in Austin, Texas.

"The University of Texas proposed it," Nolan explained, "and they asked if I would be in agreement with that. I certainly didn't have a problem doing it. So I told them to set it up with the Rangers. My only concern was to make sure that it didn't put Reid into an awkward position. I didn't want him to get a lot of performance anxiety over it."

Nolan thinks that Reid might have been a little bit nervous about the game. It was only natural.

Nolan Ryan — a little worse for wear — after an exhibition game against his son's college team in Austin, Texas

But the enjoyment outweighed the butterflies for Reid.

"It was just fun," Reid recalled. "I wasn't *very* nervous, because of the way my dad brought me up and because I'd been around baseball and everything. I was excited, and I wanted to do well. But I was really just going to have a good time more than anything. It was a lot of fun for everybody."

"I think that Reid looked at it as a challenge," Nolan pointed out, "and it was something he wanted to do. So I think that's really the reason that we agreed to do it."

138

Nolan pitched five innings, allowing five hits and three runs in a 12–5 win over Reid's team, the Longhorns. Reid pitched two innings, allowing five hits and four runs. The level of experience, of course, was uneven. But the college students learned a lot from facing major-leaguers, and it was a great day for all.

While Reid is working on putting up some numbers at Texas Christian University, his dad has put up a few numbers of his own. Of course, that's quite an understatement — Nolan has set 50 major league records! He played for the New York Mets, California Angels, and Houston Astros before he signed with the Texas Rangers. His many records include the number of strikeouts he has accomplished. For example, by the start of the 1992 season, Nolan had struck out a total of 5,511 batters, leading the major leagues. And Nolan has pitched more no-hitters than anyone — seven. His most recent no-hit game was a 3–0 win over the Toronto Blue Jays on May 1, 1991. The last man he retired was none other than a young baseball phenom named Roberto Alomar. It had to be a good feeling for Nolan as he fanned a player whom he remembered as a tiny child running around Anaheim Stadium with his brother, Sandy Jr.

"It's strange," Nolan admitted, when asked about playing against the offspring of former major league teammates, like the Alomar boys or Bobby Bonds' son, Barry.

"A lot of times," said Nolan, "the seasons seem

to run together. You really don't reflect on how much time has passed because you're so involved in what's going on in the present. But then you see how much other peoples' children have changed over the years. You remember them at one stage of their development, and later you see them at another. That's when you realize how much time has passed."

There are a number of father/son combos who have struck out due to Nolan's lightning-fast pitches. To date, he has fanned all of the Alomars, the Bonds, Tito and Terry Francona, the Griffeys, the McRaes, Dick and Dick Schofield, and Maury and Bump Wills. He has struck out a whole lot of major league brothers as well, like Felipe, Jesus, and Matty Alou, George and Ken Brett, Ollie and Oscar Brown, José and Hector Cruz, Tony and Chris Gwynn, Dave and Garth Iorg, Carlos and Lee May, Eddie and Rich Murray, Graig and Jim Nettles, Joe and Phil Niekro, and the Ripken brothers.

The Texas Rangers 1992 media guide lists Nolan's all-time strikeout list, which covers four pages with three lengthy columns of names on each page. As a matter of fact, Nolan's biography in the media guide alone spans 22 pages! (Most players have a bio of about three pages or less.)

Nolan also holds numerous low-hit game records. And he has had the chance to accomplish great feats in seven All-Star Games, and four Championship Series. He appeared in the 1969 World Series as a New York Met when the Mets beat the Baltimore Orioles. In 1989, Nolan became the oldest pitcher to win an All-Star Game. He was 42 at the time. Nolan has spent 25 seasons as a major leaguer. (Most players don't even play in the bigs for 20 years.) It's virtually impossible to keep one's body going for such a long time. And if a player is a starting pitcher, year after year of work can wear down the arm. Nolan was lucky enough to be born with a good, strong body, and he keeps it that way by maintaining a strict exercise regime which lasts year-round. These are the reasons why he is one of the best power pitchers of all time.

The only problem that Nolan has had in his

Nolan Ryan winds up for the pitch.

career is the tendency to sometimes be a bit wild. One of his less-noteworthy major league records is having issued the most walks, or bases on balls, with 2,686 by 1992. But one must also remember that Nolan had pitched an incredible 5,163.1 innings by that time. The typical major league pitcher hasn't spent anywhere near that amount of time on the mound. And it's a safe bet that the typical batter, when he faces Nolan Ryan, does not complacently wait for a walk. More likely, he fears that the ball will blow past him before he has had the chance to react.

While Nolan is a "flame-thrower," his son Reid has a different sort of style.

"He wasn't blessed with the same type of ability that I was," Nolan explained. "So, he has to be more of a control-style pitcher, and get his breaking ball over, and work on his change-up."

There's no question that Reid adores the game of baseball. Time will tell how far the game takes him. But for now, Reid knows that it's very important to work hard in school. He majors in radio, television, and film at Texas Christian.

"I would like to play baseball as long as I can," Reid said. "But when I get done with that, I want to do something in television. I haven't decided what aspect yet, whether it will be broadcasting and being in front of the camera, or whatever. But I'd like to stay with sports, and do something in that area."

With an inspirational father like Nolan, it's easy to see why Reid would be interested in sports broadcasting. On several occasions, Reid has accompanied his father on road trips, where he can get into a uniform and play catch with Nolan's teammates. When Reid and his siblings were little, Nolan took time out whenever he could to play ball with them.

"My dad's been great," Reid said. "He's always made special time for us."

Nolan has proven to be a good role model for his children. Reid says that Nolan has always told them to treat others with respect. He has also stressed the ideas of trying and working hard, no matter what his kids decide to do in life.

"If you work hard and do your best," Reid observed, "there's not much more people can ask of you. So that's kind of the way I've carried my life."

And given the successful road that Nolan Ryan has taken, it couldn't be a better idea to take his advice.

Conclusion

Baseball or Not — Use What You've Got!

Although it would be a lot of fun to have the chance to play major league baseball, let's face it: not everyone was born to do it. But just like Cal Ripken, Jr., pointed out, everyone is good at something. And the key to life is that you should make the most out of what you have. Just do your best, and see what happens.

"It's hard to get that point across," said Cal Ripken, Jr., "because you don't see the benefits of being in school the way you see the benefits of being in baseball. But baseball is only going to take you so far, and then after that, the important way to deal with that is to be educated. That's how I feel about it."

Todd Stottlemyre couldn't agree more.

"When you're ten or twelve years old," said Todd, "sometimes you'd rather be doing some-

144

thing else than going to school. As I got older, I enjoyed school more. There's no substitute for education. There's no doubt about it, it's the smart thing to do. Stay in school and do well."

Cal Ripken, Jr., is involved in a literacy program in the Baltimore area. He says that there are a lot of people out there who do not know how to read. And that is a very difficult way to get through life.

"You take it for granted," said Cal, on knowing how to read. "If you're on a plane, killing time, and you want to learn something, you can just get a magazine and read. And people who haven't learned how to read have had to drop out of school. So you really start understanding the importance of an education."

When Julian Javier played in St. Louis, he used to visit the schools in the area and talk to kids about the importance of a good education.

"I told them about everything," said Julian. "About drugs, and not drinking, and being good in school. So forget about the drugs, and don't get together with all those guys who have a bad reputation. Stay clean, study hard, and finish school. Maybe you could make it to be a good lawyer, a good doctor, or something like that."

"All the advice I can give to kids," said Roberto Alomar, "is to say away from the bad places, and stay in the right line."

School does not only involve cracking the books. It actually has a lot more to offer than that. "I think that without an education," said Sandy

Alomar, Sr., "you can't go anywhere. School will teach you how to do a lot of things. It will teach you how to deal with people, and how to handle things. You have to learn about all the different ways of life."

A college education is not always something that a person chooses, or can afford. But a lot of the players agree that, if possible, kids should try to go to college. There's even more to learn there.

"I'm not really a person to ever look back and say that I wish I could change anything," said Todd Stottlemyre, "but if there was one thing I could do, that would be to go out and get my college education."

"You see, baseball and any sport can be so short," Roberto Alomar pointed out. "And you don't know where you're going to be after that. So, you have to go to college and get a degree. I think that's one of the best things you can do. I didn't do it, because I was young [when he signed]. But if I didn't make it, I could go back to school."

José Tartabull talks to his players about the necessity of education whenever he gets the chance. It's a subject that is too important to ignore. "I say, Hey, sometime, you guys, if you haven't finished college, go ahead. If you have any time to finish the degree that you started — even in the off-season — don't be afraid to finish."

Brian McRae recognizes that fact. He signed out of high school, but that certainly doesn't mean that the idea of college is closed to him.

"That's still an option for me," said Brian. "When I get done playing ball, I'll go back to school to pursue some other career or other venture afterwards."

Brian already has an interesting career idea in mind. He was going to be a radio and TV broadcasting major in college. So, he will look into the communications area someday after he is retired.

Mel Stottlemyre, Sr., thinks that it's a safe bet to have a back-up career goal planned, just in case the first doesn't work out. Especially for young baseball players who may need to turn to another field when their time in baseball runs out.

"I think that if they have that educational background," explained Mel Sr., "it's a great feeling for them to know that they don't really *have* to succeed at this sport to do well. I think anytime, whether it's a player or another person, if they have another thing to fall back on, it makes it much easier. There's much less pressure on them."

Bob Boone is very thankful that he and those in his family have had the chance to go to college. In their case, their baseball talents helped them there, too. Bob and his sons, Bret and Aaron, were given baseball scholarships to attend Stanford and USC, respectively. Both boys are close to graduating.

"When I look back on my life," said Bob, "the four years I spent at Stanford are a huge part of it. I'm really proud of my sons being in baseball, but I'm also very proud of the fact that they got deep into a college education. To me, a big part of the college experience is just that — the *college experience*. It's the educational experience that broadens us. It makes us better people. I think it's almost impossible to measure. I'm very grateful to baseball because it's given my family a chance to be educated."

The important thing to realize is that it's never too late. After all, human beings go on learning new things for the rest of their lives. There is no one age that someone stops learning. For example, Ken Griffey, Sr., who now does color commentary for Seattle Mariners games, has spent some time at the University of Phoenix learning about the communications field. It was a perfect opportunity for him to learn more about his new job, especially the interviewing techniques and the technical side of television.

His son, Ken Jr., was always interested in art and plans to design his own house one day. Stanley Javier has the same type of interest in architecture, but is not sure if he will pursue it when he is no longer playing baseball. But he always thought that if he didn't get the chance to be a ballplayer, he would have been an architect. Sometimes on road trips, he takes special notice of the buildings in the major league cities he visits. "I always liked to draw," Stanley said. "I like to scratch on paper and create things. I just always liked that career."

Danny Tartabull has a few ideas of what he

might like to do someday after baseball. "When I was younger," said Danny, "I was very much involved in wanting to be an air traffic controller. But as I've gotten older, I've realized that my talents are more into the real estate field. For sure, when I'm done with baseball, I'll own a real estate company."

Danny loved school when he was a kid.

"School was a place where I could manifest myself in many ways," Danny said, "and see my friends. Schoolwork to me was never a problem. One of my favorite subjects was history. I like reading about history and going on trips and actually seeing the history of different things. I enjoy museums and I enjoy tours, things of that nature."

Sandy Alomar, Jr., has numerous interests. He loves to work with his hands. He loves computers, especially laptops. And he really enjoys looking at and learning about the world around him.

"If I weren't a ballplayer," Sandy Jr. said, "I would probably be in science. I would love to work for NASA, or *try* to work for them. I don't know."

When Sandy was a little boy, he had a great ambition to be an airline pilot.

"I liked it," said Sandy, "but then, I lost interest in it. I'm a curious guy. I like dangerous things, like riding dirt bikes, and this and that. I just love planes. When I was a kid, I would look at a plane and think, How can this metal plane be in the air? How can this big old bird fly? You know, it's elements, air, lift, engine, design, speed. And I really like all that stuff."

So there are a lot of different options out there for people to explore. Jesus Alou is glad that he was — and is — in baseball. But even though his son, Jesus (Jay) Jr., is 6-feet-2-inches tall and weighs a healthy 190 pounds, he won't be seen on a major league baseball diamond.

"He's not going to be a ballplayer," Jesus said. "That was one thing I missed, having that full education. And when I had my boy, I made up my mind that he was going to have an education. At the age of 24, he's still involved in books. I believe education is very important. Even though I was a big league player for such a long time, I would right now trade all that for a degree. That's how I see it."

Jay Jr. is currently going to school to be a doctor, having just graduated from Eckerd College.

"So he's got quite some time before he makes it to the big leagues in *that* profession," said Jesus with a smile.

Jesus Alou's brother Matty feels that school is just one place where you can get an education. Family life is extremely significant, too. Maria, Virginia, Juan, Felipe, Jesus, and Matty Alou were brought up very well by their parents, Virginia and José.

"I come from a poor family," Matty explained. "But our mother always took care of us. We got our education from our home, from our mother especially. So, the first thing is to have a mother and a father. And school comes second."

Education comes from many different schools and many different places. It's just a matter of finding what you like. And when you find it, stick with it, and try to do the very best at it. And if you haven't found it yet, don't worry. With time and thought, it will come to you. Just work hard and try to do well at everything. And soon your talent will emerge. When it does, take good care of it. Because it will be different from everyone else's.

It's really the same way with these baseball players. They found what they wanted, some early on in life, some a bit later. And the only reason they made it is simple — they *tried*. Their family names are just something they received at birth. More importantly, their *families* provided them with love and support, no matter what profession they chose.

Bibliography

Neft, David S., and Richard M. Cohen, eds. *The Sports Encyclopedia, Baseball, 1992 Edition*. New York: St. Martin's Press, 1989.

Thorn, John, Pete Palmer, and David Reuther, eds. *Total Baseball, Second Edition*. New York: Warner Books, 1989, 1991.